REFEREEING 1,000 FIGHTS

PORTRAIT OF THE AUTHOR. *Bassano Photo.*

Frontispiece.

REFEREEING 1,000 FIGHTS

REMINISCENCES OF BOXING

BY
EUGENE CORRI

WITH FOREWORD BY
THE EARL OF LONSDALE

LONDON
C. ARTHUR PEARSON, LTD.,
HENRIETTA STREET, W.C. 2.
1919

The First Edition of this book was published in 1915 *under the title*
THIRTY YEARS A BOXING REFEREE.
Second Edition 1919.

FOREWORD

MY DEAR MR CORRI,—I have always considered that boxing really combines all the finest and highest inclinations of a man—activity, endurance, science, temper, and, last, but not least, presence of mind. I mean, of course, boxing under legitimate and honest conditions, governed by those who are above suspicion and have no axe to grind—they are the ones who conduce most to the really *bona fide* and legitimate game and science of boxing.

In days gone by the boxing community was of a very different type, and had a different surrounding, from that of the present moment. The public view of boxing now is on an absolutely different standard from that of former days, and it is due to those such as yourself, through your endeavours for justice and fair play, that this extensive change of feeling has been brought about. It is, therefore, with the greatest pleasure that I send you this letter, which you are at liberty to use in your book, and I am grateful to you for informing me that you are about to produce a work setting forth to the public your large and wide experience, during the past thirty years, in connection with boxing and the Ring.

Your reminiscences will be most interesting, for there is no one who has taken a greater interest in, or been more closely allied to, all that is just and honourable in the Ring than you have, and your record as a referee alone speaks for itself.

I have had the honour of your acquaintance, and also have seen you at various contests, for many years, and it is with the greatest pleasure I learn that you consider you will be able to continue for many more years your excellent example and the interest you have so ably bestowed on your work during the past years of boxing, which now stands in a far higher position that it has ever attained in previous history. And you are one of those who have done so much to raise it to the higher standard, where really as a legitimate sport it should rank in the annals of sport.

No one, I am sure, has done more for the progress and the popularity of boxing than you have, and you have built up an international reputation as a referee, enjoying, as you do, to-day the affectionate regard of countless lovers of the sport, among whom, if I may be allowed to do so, I gladly enrol myself. Your efficiency and your unstained integrity stand, and have always stood, above any suggestion of adverse criticism.

Your services have always been so ungrudgingly given, with just the one aim—justice, fairness, and science, which, in other words, mean the good of the game; and I have no hesitation in saying that no man has done more than you have to bring about this happy consummation.

I shall read your reminiscences with the greatest interest, and sincerely trust that your book will meet with the success it deserves, for there are thousands who will read it knowing and feeling that whatever remarks you choose to make will be as just and as fair as you yourself have always been when acting as referee.

      Believe me,
        Yours very truly,
          (*Signed*) LONSDALE.

BARLEY THORPE,
 OAKHAM.

CONTENTS

CHAPTER	PAGE
INTRODUCTION	1
1. THE LUCKY-TUB OF MEMORY	11
2. THE CARPENTIER-GUNBOAT SMITH FIGHT	23
3. BOMBARDIER WELLS, WITH A WORD OR TWO ABOUT CARPENTIER	45
4. ROBERT FITZSIMMONS	80
5. WILLIE RITCHIE AND FREDDY WELSH	87
6. MATT WELLS, SERGEANT BASHAM, AND JOHNNY SUMMERS	102
7. WILDE THE WIZARD	118
8. SOME BOXING STORIES	129
9. MORE BOXING STORIES	147
10. BOXING IN THE WAR	167

LIST OF ILLUSTRATIONS

PORTRAIT OF THE AUTHOR . . *frontispiece*
GUNBOAT SMITH DELIVERING THE FATEFUL BLOW IN HIS FIGHT WITH CARPENTIER *facing page* 40
THE WELSH-RITCHIE FIGHT . . ,, 96
JIMMY WILDE AND TANCY LEE . ,, 128

REFEREEING 1,000 FIGHTS

INTRODUCTION

My chief second has whispered his final instructions into my ear, and now I know exactly what to do. And there goes the bell; the moment has come when I have got to start in earnest. And yet, truth to tell, I can hardly see the forest for trees; by that I mean that the reminiscences of three decades come tumbling into my mind so fast that it is hard to know exactly where to commence.

A longsome time, my masters—thirty years; and if one had been engaged in only the most placid of pursuits—catching the 8.35 to the City in the morning, and returning, as a dutiful husband should, by the 6.18 to wife and suburbia—there would be yarns worth telling. Then how much more is that the case when the record deals with a score and a half of years spent in the vivid and vital atmosphere of boxing! Now, if only I could just sit down and yarn away with a smart stenographer to jot it down, the job might come easier to me, for this pen-and-paper business is just a little trying. You must make allowances. You will not get an orderly review, the events of one year nicely disposed of before the events of the next are tackled. I am not writing "the story of my life" as the phrase is generally understood; I am just dipping into the lucky-tub of memory, and I hope for your sake and for mine that the prizes will outnumber the blanks. For my sake, I say, for, after all, there will be pleasure for me. I shall once again be in the company of dear old friends now "gone West"; once again I and they will pass the time together.

As a matter of fact, I should not have listened to my friends when they urged me to write this book had it not been for the prospect of living over again the days that have gone. Ah, those memories of men and things!—a touch of sadness about it all, maybe, but who will deny that there is not pleasure, too?

When my friends are in a genial mood they tell me that I have done my "bit" for boxing. Well, that is as it may be, but certain it is that boxing has done a very big bit for me. My happiest memories are all associated with the great game. I suppose that every man who attains a certain age, when he looks at the backward stretch of years, says to himself that had he to live his life over again he would have this and that different. I am no exception, but the one thing I certainly would not have different is my connection with boxing. Need I tell you that I think it is the greatest of all sports? I have always said, and thought, that if a fellow has a real, genuine love of boxing, it is long odds that he is a white man at bottom, for there is something in boxing that shames the little shabby meannesses out of a man; there is a great big humanity about it all—precious little sentiment, but a flavour of warm-hearted comradeship, surely one of the things to make life worth while.

I am not out to throw bouquets, but if there is a more likeable lot of good fellows than the boxing army I would vastly appreciate an introduction to that select coterie. Anyway, boxers and boxing men are good enough for the present humble scribe.

Glancing back, I can recall precious few instances in which a beaten boxer has clearly begrudged the winner the spoils of victory; but I can recall hundreds of cases in which men in the first moments of defeat —and they are very bitter moments to a boxer— have put the proper feeling into their grip of their opponent's hand. Generosity in sport is everything; if we are to have spite and envy, then it's a bad sport that breeds those feelings, and we are better without it.

There is something very simple and primitive about boxing, and it is the simple virtues that its devotees admire; and boxing is British all the way through. In Germany the apostles of "Kultur" have always fought against the popularisation of boxing, and the rank and file of the people have had little liking for the game. We can appreciate the reason why now.

Boxing is a game for men, and only for men, We who are in it like the company we keep, and maybe are proud of it, although we do not say much about that. We have no use for sycophants or time-servers, and I think most of us recognize real manliness when we see it.

I said that boxing has done a big bit for me. One of the best things it has done has been to make me admire pluck and courage. Don't let me frighten you; I am not going to moralize or pose as a philosopher. But I'll just say this : I am a youngster no longer; I have seen all sorts and conditions of men in all sorts of odd circumstances; I have had moments—many moments—when life has come to me with the veneer off, and I have learned, I hope, the great thing—not to be afraid of life, to take your fun and your sorrows with a laugh. If it's fun— well, enjoy it, boys; if it's sorrow, we will hope for better luck. A plain philosophy, you say? That may be, but not a bad one in this workaday world. There are many worse ones, with long names, expounded by far cleverer men than I. Oh, we're not a subtle crowd in boxing, but, once again, I am proud of the friendships I have made in the game.

Sport—and boxing particularly—knows no social distinctions, and even the "colour" line is not drawn. There are men among the actual participants in the game whom I feel honoured to know—fellows who ring true all the way through. A few black sheep? Why, of course. But, believe me, the

INTRODUCTION 5

proportion is not high among boxers, and the gentlemen who are so crooked that they could sleep in a corkscrew soon find their level—and it is a pretty low one always. The old trite saying that "Honesty is the best policy" is absolutely true in boxing. There have been men who have preferred the other thing, but their reign has been neither long nor successful.

What of the game and its progress or retrogression in thirty years ? It would be simply folly for me to write that boxers are more clever, or less clever, to-day than they were thirty years ago. Large generalizations like that are always misleading.

But what I can say is, that boxing is very, very different from boxing as I first knew it—I mean the whole atmosphere of the game. Great sporting days, those of thirty years ago! And yet, when I put the question fairly and squarely to myself whether it would be a good thing for boxing if those days were to return, I can only say, "No."

There were elements in the game then that were not conducive to boxing becoming the great national sport it is to-day. I, for one, would always fight against boxing being so "refined" that the simple hardiness of it all is lost; and yet that does not blind me to the fact that a man of sensitive temperament ought to be able to see and enjoy boxing. He can, and does, do so to-day. A fellow whose susceptibilities are hurt by boxing as it is conducted at, say, the National Sporting Club, is altogether too good for this world; he ought to spend his days reading love-sonnets or knitting antimacassars. It is true that we still see what the old-timers loved to call "the claret" flow, but is there anything very shocking in that?

Ah, those old-timers! Rough, uncouth fellows? Yes, all that, if you will; but he is a better man who can read of some of their exploits and admire them. I like to think of that battle in which the "Game Chicken" was engaged. I forget the name of his opponent, but that does not matter. They battled on for many rounds until they were both on the verge of complete exhaustion, and then nature gave way with one of them, and he fell, an inert, helpless mass of quivering flesh. And the winner tottered across the ring, and, shaking the hand of the man who had been battering him almost senseless, he shouted: "You're a damned fine fellow!"

If you can picture that scene and then shrug your shoulders in supercilious scorn of such "brutal" men, well, quite frankly, I am sorry for you.

And yet I would repeat that the Ring is better without some of the "atmosphere" of the old days. In the palmy days of the Prize Ring, during the Regency, it was the hangers-on who brought the sport into disrepute. And thirty years ago the successors of these hangers-on were still rather too much in evidence. A little sporting wager on the chances of a boxer is one thing; the game turned into a medium for huge gambles is very much another.

INTRODUCTION

Money talks all languages, and in the past it often talked the language of "fake" in boxing. We are all the better for being without that aspect of the game.

The past is always picturesque, for the backward view lends the magic of enchantment, and we see things perhaps not quite as they really were. But while I pay ungrudging tribute to the cleverness of those old-time men of the Ring, and while I am full of admiration for their matchless courage and splendid endurance, I still think that boxing—viewed as a great national sport—was never in a healthier state than it is to-day.

And now let me say a few things on the broad aspects of referees and refereeing. I don't want to educate you—the Fates forbid that I should be so presumptuous!—and still less do I wish to bore you. But everything that follows will have some connection with my life as a referee, so it cannot be out of place to deal for a moment with general principles.

If I said I had refereed a thousand fights I suppose I should be somewhere near the mark. If I were asked to summarize my experience, gained in thirty years, and give a word of advice to referees, it would be this: The referee must be the most important personage of the trio—the two boxers and himself—and yet he must be the least conspicuous. An officious referee is a bad referee—not sometimes, but all the time. Yet there must be no possible misunderstanding about his position. He is the man on top—the "boss," if you like to put it so ; and the boxers must know and appreciate that fact beyond all doubt.

Knowledge of the game there must be, of course, and a capacity for quick thinking and prompt, decisive action. But something else is required—personality. The boxers must be made to feel that they can take no liberties ; if they feel that, they will act accordingly, and the task of the referee is made correspondingly lighter. And the referee, in a sense, must be "on top" even where the crowd is concerned. Nothing so incenses a boxing gathering as a busybody of a referee ; but given quiet methods and a knowledge of your job, and it is in the last degree unlikely that you will encounter serious trouble from the crowd.

Let me give you an instance of what I mean, and please do not think that I am singing my own praises. When Gunboat Smith and Carpentier met at Olympia on that memorable July night a few days before Europe was plunged into war, there were all the elements of trouble when the American got himself disqualified. Into the merits of my decision I am not going now ; what I want to point out is that the one fatal thing would have been indecision. In this connection I might well adapt a famous saying to the business of refereeing, and put it that : "You can please some of the people all the time ; you can please all the people some of the time ; but you can't please all the people all the time." No, you very certainly can do nothing of the kind, and a referee who tries to accomplish that miracle is on the turnpike road leading to trouble.

He is not there to please anybody, and until he has thoroughly digested that fact he will have quite a lot to learn. He is there to do just one thing : to administer the laws of boxing, and to use his discretion and judgment as to what latitude he shall allow the men, for the laws of boxing are not as the laws of the Medes and Persians ; if they were, there would be a plethora of very brief contests, I am afraid.

I trust I am not an unduly assertive man, and yet I must admit that a little of the quarter-deck style is not out of place when the job on hand is refereeing a boxing contest. I am told that there is singularly little of the " Whisper and I shall hear " business about my orders to two boxers. Well, it won't do, you know ! It is necessary to get your orders into a very few words, and it is as well if you say those words as if you mean them.

In one respect, and that an important one, the English boxing referee is in a position that is unique. He is accountable to no authority apart from the tribunal of public opinion. Opinions, it is easy to understand, may differ as to whether this fact makes for the good of the game. But it is clear that while this is the state of affairs it is absolutely imperative that the integrity of the referee should be—like Cæsar's wife—above suspicion. If it is not, then the public are going to lose faith in the game, and boxing would suffer enormously.

So much by way of what may be termed the Introductory Note. Now you must let me "gang my ain gait." Really, the pace ought not to be slow, for my life has not been dull, and queer folks, and queerer things, have passed my way. For the nonce I can give free play to memory, for I am writing this in the period when Throgmorton Street, which has for so long been my centre, is what Mr Mantalini would have called a "demned dirty dismal place," thanks to the war. And being "out of work," I will live over again some of those thirty years of refereeing which have been the happiest and most instructive and educative, in the real sense of the word, of my life.

CHAPTER I

THE LUCKY-TUB OF MEMORY

Two pairs of sleeve-links and a ring—Johnny Summers and his cross—What Gunboat Smith said—A fight at Wells's Club.

THERE are two ways in which a man may tell the story of his life : he may adopt the method of an architect who prepares a careful plan for the builder, or he may adopt the haphazard method—call it, rather, the happy-go-lucky method—of the storyteller who rattles on in his own way as incidents and ideas arise in his mind.

That will be my method.

I shall tax my memory to recall the brightest episodes of my long career as a referee of boxing in all departments of the noble art, amateur and professional ; or, better still, I shall stand aside and catch the contents of memory as they are poured forth.

As I have said, I must have refereed no fewer than a thousand fights during my thirty years at the game ; besides this, I must have witnessed three times as many more.

I am concerned strictly to stick to facts, as, indeed, I have no occasion to resort to invention or exaggeration. Besides being stranger than fiction, truth is funnier than fiction. I am sure it will be difficult for me to do full justice to myself and to all the many sportsmen and fighting men whose names will appear in course of my reminiscences.

The scenes I have witnessed, and the sayings I have heard, will require more than the storytelling ability which I possess to recount them in all their original vividness.

Sportsmen as a class are breezy in their manners and expressive in their speech. If I were to try to improve upon the many merry and bright jests which have thrown me and my friends into fits of laughter, my efforts could only result in spoiling the point. It must, therefore, be my object to prove a faithful and frank recorder, so that you, my readers, may live over again with me the brightest parts of my sporting past.

On this understanding, then, I step into the ring, so to speak, to give battle to my memory, jolting it and jogging it about, so that nothing worth remembering shall be omitted or forgotten.

At the moment of writing my eye glances from the page before me to my shirt-cuffs, where I see, not without a conscious feeling of vanity, a pair of dainty and original links, which were presented to me—it seems only the other day—by my friend Mr C. B. Cochran, as a memento of the great fight between Georges Carpentier and the American giant, Gunboat Smith.

THE LUCKY-TUB OF MEMORY 13

Mr Cochran had frequently mentioned that he meant to give me something unique. He succeeded admirably in this kind intention. The links to which I have referred are in the form of miniature boxing-gloves, mounted in platinum and studded with diamonds. We are all boys, whatever the calendar may say to the contrary; I believe we are at our best as men when the boyish mood is upon us. The remark of a sporting friend was not wide of the mark when, upon my showing him Mr Cochran's present to me, he said, " Gene, you are as vain as a boy about these links. I believe your only trouble is that the sleeves of your shirt are rather too short to show them to full advantage." I suppose he had noticed me pulling the cuffs into view to feast my own eyes upon the links.

One thing suggests another, and, as the habitual storytellers of our acquaintance say, " that reminds me " of another story about links, which are worn to-day, with as much pride as I wear mine, by Packy Macfarland, the famous American light-weight. A few years ago the commanding officer at Shoeburyness Garrison asked me whether I could bring a champion down with me for the entertainment of the soldiers. I said I should do the best I could, and I had no difficulty in the world in securing this favour from Packy Macfarland, who not only gave his services free, but pooh-poohed all mention of having his expenses defrayed. Your first-class boxing man is very often a pure sportsman, who dearly loves to exhibit this quality. He is also, generally speaking, a gentleman in all the essentials of that exalted term. The officers at Shoeburyness were charmed with Packy Macfarland, as indeed they well might be, for no man could better behave than Packy, in any company, however superior or exacting. The young pugilist's unassuming manners, his cleverness with the gloves, his uncomplaining willingness to do as much sparring as the men cared to ask him for, the thorough style in which he punished all comers, while taking the precaution of not knocking out or seriously injuring anyone, so impressed his antagonists and his audience that, with one consent, they voted Packy to be the best of good fellows. The commanding officer invited him to dine in the mess, and put him up at the barracks for the night. You can always trust a British officer for hospitality. Not only was Packy Macfarland entertained in this handsome manner, but he was afterwards presented with the loveliest pair of links he ever set his eyes on, which derived a special distinction and value from the fact that they were stamped with the regimental badge. The young boxer assured me that of all his many trophies and presents, none would be valued more by him than this souvenir of Shoeburyness.

I have not done with jewellery yet. As I told you, I propose to tell the story of my career just as it occurs to me, hoping thereby best to please you and best to please myself. A day or two ago I met a comparative stranger at Westcliff-on-Sea ; he knew

THE LUCKY-TUB OF MEMORY 15

me better than I knew him. I suppose I may claim to have an enormously wide circle of acquaintances in consequence of the conspicuous place it has been my privilege to fill for a generation in the sporting world. This gentleman came up to me, and in the course of conversation showed me a solid gold plain ring which belonged to the late Tom Sayers. I have that ring on my finger now. I could not dissuade my friend from placing it there. He did not ask me to buy it, and I did not hurt his feelings by making any offer for it. He wanted me to have it, as he thought that on my hand it would be appropriately worn, and already many of my sporting friends to whom I have shown the ring have examined it with admiring, if not with covetous, eyes.

On 23rd September 1914 I went again to Shoeburyness, on the occasion of a boxing entertainment at the barracks, and again I took with me a champion, this time Johnny Summers, the premier welter-weight of England. Bombardier Wells would have come also, but he was prevented by his first-born's birthday party falling on the same day. Wells dotes on his baby boy, and could have been seen nursing him at the window on the morning after his one-round defeat by Carpentier, no doubt deriving solace to his wounded feelings in his paternal pride.

Owing to the war, some restrictions had been placed upon the liberties of the men, who were required to be in Shoeburyness Barracks several hours earlier than during peace times. In after years we shall all be telling how clubs and public-houses were closed by law during the Great War as early as nine o'clock at night, without serious protest on the part of the people, who trusted the authorities to know their own business best and to be doing everything for the national good. It is characteristic of the British temperament to keep cool in all circumstances, and to preserve our inborn love of sport, even while the bloody game of war was being played on the fields of the Continent.

The officers at Shoeburyness decided to relieve the monotony of garrison life by getting up a boxing function for the benefit of the men doing defensive duty and preparing for whatever work the War Office might, at a moment's notice, call upon them to do. Fond as soldiers are of football, I have always found them fonder still of fighting, which, by the way, is very much in their line, especially when their country is at war. I witnessed some excellent boxing on the part of the Shoeburyness men, and Johnny Summers never tired of giving them, his challengers, a taste of the best that was in him. He refrained at will from knocking any of them out, but I imagine some of them would feel the stinging after-effects of his blows for days to come. Summers is the quietest little fighting gentleman in the world. He talks very little, but is a most excellent listener to any good stories that are going. With myself, he dined with the officers afterwards, and they put him up for the night.

Johnny is a devout Catholic, and he carries his

religion into his work in a manner that is remarkable. While training he invariably keeps beside him in his quarters a pocket crucifix, to which he has recourse at frequent intervals. The crucifix may be concealed under a pillow, as was the case at Brighton when training to fight Freddy Welsh at the National Sporting Club several years ago, or it may be skilfully concealed in his sock, where it can be reverently touched at will.

I am reminded of a funny story in connection with Johnny's religious observances at the National Sporting Club. On that occasion he very noticeably crossed himself at the start of a severe contest with Jimmy Britt, and then characteristically "crossed his opponent" with his right hand.

After the bout Britt, who was always a humorist, came to me and said—I give his very words: "Mr Corri, I am satisfied with your decision." I had given the verdict to Summers. "The only thing I did not like about the contest was that habit of Summers in making the sign of the cross at the commencement of every round—appealing to the Almighty to give a guy like me a hiding. But I do not think He can be very fond of him, because Summers never hurt me."

A friend of mine who spoke to Summers on one occasion about this devout practice of his, said that the boxer took it all in good part, and openly avowed that it did him good and helped him at his work. "Fighting is my profession," said Summers, "and

I am not ashamed of it. If I introduce my religion into my daily occupation, it is no more than every Catholic ought to do. Some people look down upon boxing as coarse and brutalizing; if that is what they see in it, I am afraid there must be something coarse and brutal about themselves. I call it manly, and in no way demoralizing; and as I think of it, so is it to me." There you have a great secular sermon in a very few words from the lips of a boxer: " Nothing is either good or bad, but thinking makes it so."

I have made a passing allusion to the dramatic fight between Gunboat Smith and Georges Carpentier. I shall have a good deal more to say about this fight later on, but let me tell you a story which greatly amused the officers at Shoeburyness when I told it to them. Mr James White, the well-known financier and sportsman, drove me out to see Smith at his training quarters at Harrow-on-the-Hill. There he was, sporting about on the lawn in front of his hotel, with his black trainer, good-natured Bob Armstrong, trying to urge a goat on to spar with the Gunboat.

"How do you do?" said Smith. "I am glad to see you, Mr Corri. So you're going to referee the fight?"

Then, stooping, he laid his hands on my shoulders and looked me square in the face, saying: " Let me look in your eyes, Mr Corri. I like a referee with a pair of good lights in his head. Yours look good and all right." I told him I hoped so, and that he would have no occasion to think otherwise after the fight.

"I have never seen that French guy," said Gunboat, "but when I meet him at Olympia I shall bring a right-hand punch right over from my hip, and if I land on that French guy he will think Olympia has fallen in. So look out for that punch, Mr Corri, and mind you keep out of its way in case it goes wide."

Smith did not land that punch so far as I saw, and I was nearer the fighters than anybody else, being in the ring beside them. Olympia did not fall; Gunboat Smith did, and if I am not mistaken the American champion was very glad to take the count to the ninth second in the fourth round.

Another story which amused the officers related to an experience I had when refereeing at Shoeburyness on the first occasion. Two men were boxing very badly in the novices' competition; neither had any idea of correct hitting; both were swinging their arms like semaphores and missing each other in an amusing manner. At last one man managed to hit his opponent on the back of the head, delivering what sporting writers call the "occipital blow." The man who received it immediately put up his hand to his head with an expression of the most comical distress on his face, and called out: "'E's done it, 'e's done it, 'e's done it!"

I looked at him and said: "What do you mean by saying, ' 'E's done it'?"

The only answer I got was, "I'll retire," as the fellow bolted through the ropes like a rabbit, while the audience shrieked with laughter.

During the war the casualty lists contained the names of many officers and men who were well known to me in the sphere of fisticuffs. My eyes moistened to read of the death of that splendid young officer, Captain Norman de Crespigny. I knew Norman de Crespigny well.

Once I refereed an impromptu fight in which he was one of the combatants. His opponent on that occasion was Captain Rome of the 11th Hussars, who held among other honours the Public Schools Championship.

The scene of this sporting match was Wells's Club, and it will always rank as the one incident of my life with which I can compare no other.

Captain Rome chanced to mention that he had a good boy in his regiment who weighed nine stone four, and he said he would match him against any other boy in the army for a side bet of a hundred pounds. Young Captain de Crespigny replied : "I have a good boy in my regiment, and I don't mind matching him against yours, Captain Rome."

Accordingly the match took place without delay at Wells's Club, one of the most select and best-appointed social sporting clubs in the world. The men were matched to box the best of six rounds, and it was a fine ding-dong battle. I gave the verdict to Captain Rome's boy.

THE LUCKY-TUB OF MEMORY 21

That same evening, shortly after this contest, Captain de Crespigny walked up to Captain Rome, and said : " I am perfectly satisfied your man won right enough. It would be a bit of sport if we two now had a go—a fitting climax, so to speak, to the evening's amusement."

Without a moment's hesitation Captain Rome agreed, and immediately the two officers divested themselves of their evening-dress shirts and boxed in their undervests, as amateurs always do. I was again appointed referee, and for the first two or three rounds I thought de Crespigny was beaten, except that one could not fail to have some hope for a man who so pluckily took the hiding he was getting.

Rome was probably heavier by two or three stone. Then, as often happens in boxing, young de Crespigny warmed to his work in the fourth round, and knocked Captain Rome clean out with as fine a right-hand punch in the chin as anybody could wish to see.

There was great excitement in Wells's Club that night. I suppose there would be about a hundred gentlemen present, including a fair sprinkling of the younger members of the nobility. I refereed both bouts, and stayed behind to a grand supper in celebration of the occasion.

The two officers who had fought so finely sat next each other at the table, chatting as gaily and eating as heartily as if neither had just been strenuously employed pummelling the other.

This happened only about a month before the

outbreak of the war, and I suppose not more than half those present that night could have been brought together again while the war lasted.

Alas for young Norman de Crespigny ! He will never return. He will long be remembered by his brother officers and all who, like myself, had the pleasure of his acquaintance, as the purest of sportsmen and the brightest and best of young Britons.

On that eventful night Sir Claud de Crespigny seconded his son, and the weight of his bereavement can well be imagined. He did not grudge his son to his country's cause, but the grand old sportsman's loss must have been well-nigh insupportable. No patriotism is deeper than that of the English sporting squire, and no heart is kindlier.

Havoc of the war !

How many gaps it has torn in the family circles of our old English nobility !

CHAPTER II

THE CARPENTIER—GUNBOAT SMITH FIGHT

POSSIBLY the two greatest fights, considered from a spectacular point of view, which I ever refereed were the contest between Freddy Welsh and Willie Ritchie for the light-weight championship of the world, and that between Gunboat Smith and Georges Carpentier for the heavy-weight championship of the world in the ranks of white men. Jack Johnson's claim to be the world's champion stood then an undisputed and incontestable fact.

Both the fights to which I have referred took place at Olympia, London, during the great boxing boom which came immediately before the war. It was a curious coincidence that the British nation should have suddenly manifested such unusual enthusiasm for this robust form of sport, on the eve of the greatest struggle in our history.

How many of the young men, and even those who can no longer be called young, found themselves a few months afterwards serving their King and country on the Continent! Only the other day I talked with one of London's leading tailors in Saville Row about the war, its general effect upon the trade of the country, and especially upon tailoring.

"It has been a knock-out for me," said the fashionable tailor. He took me into his shop, and there showed me a typewritten list of between two and three hundred naval and military customers then at the front. He called it his Roll of Honour. Opposite the names of those reported killed and missing he had put a black cross. I counted eighty-one, and identified many with boxing in the Army and the Navy.

"I suppose," said the tailor, "these fellows spent with me on the average anything from two hundred pounds to three hundred pounds a year on clothes. You can imagine the effect upon my turn-over of the withdrawal of this volume of custom. That is a selfish way of speaking, but I am only stating facts."

. . . . . .

The fame of Gunboat Smith preceded him to London, which he was visiting for the first time. His resounding title and the "tall" stories about him with which the American press had regaled the sporting world, ensured for him a great reception on his arrival in the Metropolis. Thousands of people congregated in and around Paddington Station, and made his entry a triumphal one.

The Gunboat, as he stepped from his carriage, looked abashed at the crowd cheering and gesticulating about him. His young wife, who accompanied him, gazed like a timid fawn upon the scene, and no

CARPENTIER AND GUNBOAT SMITH

doubt felt prouder than ever of her hero-husband. The Gunboat had to make a speech, interspersed with the usual picturesque slang of his class.

Interviewers pounced upon him with their notebooks and pencils in readiness. He said all the things he was expected to say—the sort of things that fellow-countrymen like Jeffries and Corbett had said before him. Like all other heavy-weight pugilists, he towered head and shoulders above his surging admirers, and was freely photographed as a giant among comparative pigmies. London read the story next day of the great man's arrival, and doubtless many very nice people smiled at the affair as out of all proportion to its importance. But there you are. Great boxers always have been, and very likely always will be, quite as popular as Princes of the blood. Their popularity is neither very deep nor very lasting. It does not win for them a pedestal at Madame Tussaud's. The commotion they cause has the distinction of being unequalled in the realm of sport, and, that being their particular world, it is no doubt very gratifying to them. We do not accord such receptions to individual footballers or cricketers, and why this should be I am unable to explain, except by the simple process of pointing to the fact and saying that it is so.

My first meeting with Gunboat Smith was at the Waldorf Hotel, when he met the Sporting Press of London at a formal reception. The assembled pressmen were well impressed, and I imagine that the majority saw in the Gunboat a man who would avenge the double defeat of Bombardier Wells by inflicting a reverse upon Carpentier.

He had, indeed, all the appearance of a champion, except for one weak feature in his face, which was noted at the time. His nose lacked the bridge of a conqueror, and set one wondering whether he had the force of character to cope with Carpentier. No bridge no man, you know. Brawn and muscle he possessed in abundance, unhampered by an ounce of superfluous fat. The deep-set, glaring eyes showed that he lacked nothing in temper, though no man in that room, excepting perhaps Smiler Hales, could be more amiable at a social function.

I shall always picture him on that occasion, standing in the front of the company, like a man who had some difficulty in knowing what to do with his long arms, long legs, and decidedly big feet in a stationary posture. I am sure he regarded that reception as a necessary evil, and would very much have preferred to have squatted anywhere on a chair, with his legs thrown over another one, in the company of two or three personal friends.

My old friend, Mr John M. Dick, had the deserved honour of welcoming the Gunboat to England on behalf of the London Sporting Press. Mr Dick said all the right things in his own happy way, and emphasized the great point that Englishmen would give all credit to America if Gunboat Smith should beat Carpentier. " We were," he said, " jealous for the reputation of the noble art, and ready at all times to acclaim with unstinted applause any white man who proved himself to be a masterly exponent of its science."

Whatever were the hopes of the newspaper men, good judges every one, I surmised that most of them expected Gunboat Smith to win. Mr Dick Burge, the promoter of the contest, was so thoroughly satisfied of this that he backed Smith for five hundred pounds, and after the fight admitted to me that he had proved to be a poor judge on that occasion. One of the first to speak to me after I had given my much-debated decision against Smith was Mr J. B. Joel, who had lost a bet of four hundred pounds. He said: "Corri, that is the finest decision you ever gave, and I liked the way you stood firmly by your own opinion, against all the hubbub around you."

Coming as he did from America, it was necessary for Smith to get here some weeks before the fight and go into training. He stayed well out of the way at Harrow-on-the-Hill, close to the famous school, and received a fair measure of hero-worship from the boys who glided about the village, in and out the tuck-shops all day long. I recollect, on the occasion of my visiting him there, an enterprising newspaper photographer, with an eye for an effective picture, got the Gunboat to pose by the side of one of the Harrow boys, the lad blushing and the boxer grinning.

If I remember rightly, the Gunboat requested the photographer to let him have a copy of that picture, and told him that it was the only one he wanted. On another occasion Smith asked one of the boys why the regulation shell, broad-brimmed hat sat on the top of his head and fitted so badly that it required an elastic band to be worn like a reversed chin-strap that ruffled their back hair. The witty boy replied : " Because we don't like it, and it is supposed to be good for us not to get our own way."

Smith also asked him why his trousers were too short. The boy replied : " Because my legs grow downwards and my trousers shrink upwards."

The Americans have a curious way of using the word "guy." They do not intend it to convey, as we do, that a man is something of a fool or an oddity. With them it means little more than " chap " or " fellow." Smith had heard a great deal about the handsome appearance of Carpentier, and having this in his mind, one of his remarks to me was : " Mr Corri, I guess that French guy will lose his good looks when I set about him."

Carpentier trained up to date in Manitôt, only arriving in England two or three days before the fight. He came like a war hero returning home. The traffic outside Charing Cross Station, and for a considerable distance on either side of the station along the Strand, London's busiest thoroughfare, was brought to a standstill ; omnibuses, taxicabs, and vehicular traffic generally had to be diverted

CARPENTIER AND GUNBOAT SMITH

up and down adjoining streets. The reception accorded to Gunboat Smith, great as it was, compared feebly with London's welcome to the young representative from the neighbour nation across the Channel that was destined to be Britain's ally in the Great War. The fair sex mingled freely in the crowd, not unnaturally anxious to see the wonderful boy of whose physical and facial charms they had heard so much. He realized all expectations, and looked a picture of manly beauty and courage as he smiled on the semi-delirious crowd that followed him in a dense mass to his hotel in Northumberland Avenue.

No boxer of any country ever stirred the hearts of English sportsmen as did Carpentier, who had twice beaten London's pet pugilist, Bombardier Wells, and beaten him in such a way as left no doubt regarding his sportsmanship and superiority.

I met Carpentier quite accidentally at the Grand Hotel with Leon See, who subsequently became the voluntary chauffeur to General Joffre, Commander-in-Chief of the French Army. We had all met before in Paris, when I refereed the fight between the two black Sams—Langford and McVea—which took place at the Nouveau Cercle. This fight was a draw, and by a rather remarkable coincidence the same two men fought a draw in Sydney, when the great Australian sportsman, Snowy Baker, was the referee. Their third fight was fought in Melbourne, when Langford knocked McVea out, and so won the rubber.

Digressing further for a moment, I may recall that Gunboat Smith greatly enhanced his reputation by beating Langford in America, to the surprise of sportsmen everywhere, who believed that the trunky nigger was even a match for Johnson himself.

After McVea's fight with Langford I showed my card, on which I had marked points to the men as the fight proceeded, to the celebrated boxer, Porky Flynn, who was Langford's sparring partner. There was just a fraction between the aggregate of points scored by each of the men. That was possibly the first time I have ever shown my card after a fight. Flynn asked to see it, and I don't remember anybody else, not even the most pushful of interviewers, making that request.

And, of course, I asked Carpentier as to his condition. He drew upon his limited store of English to say that he was "Very well, very fit." He looked tuned to concert pitch, such a young man as it is a joy to gaze upon and a rare pleasure to meet, so charming were his manners.

He did not talk about the fight. I believe it never has been his habit to talk "shop." In private life he has always sought to escape from business affairs, like the rest of us. As for prophesying the result of the fight or boasting about what he could do, that sort of thing was not included in his code of discretion or good taste. It was too "cheap" for his patronage.

THE FIGHT

Carpentier was the first to enter the ring, accompanied by his manager, Monsieur Descamps, the spirited little Frenchman who comes as near to worshipping Carpentier as ever one man did another. I can imagine Descamps praying morning, noon and night for the safety of his darling when he, like a loyal young Frenchman, joined his fellow-countrymen in the war.

I had never before seen Carpentier look so troubled and anxious, almost nervous, as he shifted about inside the ropes waiting for his opponent, whom he, like myself, had never yet seen stripped for fighting. I fancied the Frenchman must have given some credence to the stories that had gone the round of the world, and now flooded the London press, of Gunboat Smith's reputed staggering right-hand punch, which no man, it was said, could take and remain on his feet or in his senses.

It is a habit boxers have, and especially perhaps American boxers, of beginning their battles in the papers by circulating all manner of tales of the terrible things they can do with their antagonists. I myself was looking forward with unusual interest to Smith's walloping power, wondering what I was going to see.

When the formidable Gunboat—so called by his comrades in the American Navy owing to the size of his feet—sprang into the ring and shuffled about in his curious gait, he certainly looked a dangerous fellow, and contrasted strikingly with his gentlemanly-looking young challenger.

Carpentier gave no signs whatever of being frightened. Behind his smiling mask the practised eye could easily detect indomitable resolution and unlimited confidence. The anxiety to which I have referred might perhaps be better described as a blend of curiosity and caution.

Carpentier never allows himself to presume upon his own abilities. He is impervious to flattery, and no young man ever got more in the long history of fisticuffs. I should say that he has attained to that ideal state of mental development when a man thoroughly knows himself and is able to abide firmly by his own estimate.

Instinctively I knew that Carpentier would content himself at the start to take Smith's measure before he let Smith take his. In other words, he would fight with his head to begin with, and then, having satisfied himself regarding the risks he could safely take, he would go in with gradually increasing freedom and force. To the deafening cheers that greeted him he bowed gracefully, but his thoughts were concentrated upon the business on hand.

In the great audience of fifteen thousand people— by far the most distinguished and most diversified that ever assembled to witness a boxing contest— were hundreds of Frenchmen, who went into raptures —I was going to say hysterics—as their young cham-

CARPENTIER AND GUNBOAT SMITH

pion appeared. Ladies attended in unprecedented numbers, and Carpentier was the hero of them all. Small blame to the ladies for favouring a youth so debonair, with his unblemished and perfectly regular features, his rows of gleaming white teeth, his bright eyes and golden hair brushed back from his brow in long glossy streaks.

Sportsmen from all over the country had purchased their seats weeks before, and many of the London clubs had secured boxes for their exclusive use. Peers were there in plenty, headed by Lord Lonsdale and Lord Tweedmouth. It was never positively stated that any member of the Royal Family was present, but the belief that this was so gained persistent currency.

Naturally London's resident American population attended in great numbers, and not a few made the Atlantic trip to see the fight. They might have travelled farther and fared worse. There were enough millionaires in that house to buy the German fleet. The representatives of the clergy attended, some in the conventional garb of their calling and still more in mufti—priests of both great faiths of Christendom. An American friend of mine compared the gathering to an "opera night without the opera."

Before describing the fight I should like to put on record the quizzical expression on Gunboat Smith's face and the twinkle of humour in his eyes as he looked at Carpentier, half mesmerized to see an opponent so utterly unlike in polish and deportment to any man who had ever put the gloves on to him. "That guy is a dandy," he seemed to be saying to himself, and I recollected Smith's prophecy to me that Carpentier would lose his good looks that night.

Smith unquestionably felt that the battle was as good as won already as he compared his gigantic and angular frame with the Grecian form of Carpentier. No man ever experienced—or I am grievously mistaken—such a disillusionment as Smith did when Carpentier displayed his splendid courage and consummate skill, nonplussing him from start to finish and causing the good-natured American to join the audience in laughing at his own misses and abortive lunges.

The fight started in a very business-like way. Smith sent out his left hand very low, so low that I thought it right to let him understand that blows of that kind bordered upon foul hitting. I immediately called out to him, "A little higher with your left hand, Smith."

He said, "Sorry, sir." Carpentier only smiled, and with a gesture indicated that he did not mind being hit like that. The blow had not hurt him. Speaking English, he said, "All right."

After that there was very little done in the first round of any importance, except that one could see Carpentier had satisfied himself that Gunboat Smith was not quite so dangerous a fellow as he looked. I made them even in the first round, giving each the maximum five points.

CARPENTIER AND GUNBOAT SMITH

In the second round all anxiety and curiosity had left Carpentier's face. If he were nervous to start with, his nerves had now fairly steadied, and the spectators were to see him at his splendid best. Smith's right wallop had lost its terrors, if indeed it ever had more than merely visionary terrors for the young Frenchman, who had wondered what sort of punches he was going to receive from the man whose hitting power had become notorious.

Straightway he went in to Smith and hit him when and where he liked, bamboozling the Gunboat. Once he side-stepped Smith and "made him miss" with a furious lunge which, meeting no object, threw Smith headlong on to the ropes.

I imagined Smith got out of temper here, as he commenced slinging his left hand very wildly and in a thoroughly unscientific manner. He again hit Carpentier low, and again I cautioned him. "Sorry," he growled, with that big voice of his, and scarcely so sincerely as before. Carpentier took no notice, having now thoroughly convinced himself that he had the measure of his man. Time and again he jabbed and patted Smith cleverly on the nose with his left hand, but the American's nasal organ shed very few "ruby tears." From start to finish the fight lacked sanguinary accompaniments. This was easily Carpentier's round.

At the opening of the third round the Frenchman made his opponent look like a stupefied novice, and I did not like a tactic to which Smith here resorted.

He locked Carpentier's arm in a clinch, and tried to force it up his opponent's back.

I stopped him in the nick of time, as I think. Arms are easily broken in that way. I said to him sternly, "If you do that again, Smith, I shall disqualify you." To this he made no answer, and I did not like the way he smiled. Apparently he resented my cautioning him. This was again Carpentier's round.

The opening of the fourth round saw Carpentier scoring as he liked and boxing beautifully. There was no comparison whatever between the pugilistic skill of the two men, and only a chance blow, it then appeared, could turn the tables in Smith's favour. The finest blow of the fight occurred now. Steadying himself for an instant, Carpentier landed a clean right-hand punch on the point of Smith's chin, and the Gunboat came down all of a heap like a wall.

The strong fellow managed to retain his senses, and presently got up in a sitting position. I looked at him as I counted the fateful seconds loudly in his ears. His eyes had lost their glow and his willpower was severely taxed to command his partially stunned brain.

It was impossible not to admire the indomitability of the gladiator sitting there carefully keeping count with me with the twofold object of resting himself as long as time would permit, and of making sure that he did not lose his reckoning. He kept his eyes fixed on me and on my right hand as it rose and fell.

At the ninth second Smith got upon his feet, and immediately the gong went. Everyone in the house thought the round was over, and congratulated Smith upon his "bite" of good luck. Apparently, however, the timekeeper was under the impression that he had counted Smith out. Not until after the contest did I know this.

I quite thought, as others did, that it was the end of the round. So did both the men in the ring. They had agreed that I, and only I, should count the seconds for them, in the event of either going down. Consequently their attention was fixed upon me. They did not reckon with the timekeeper at all, except in the matter of sounding the gong at the beginning and at the end of the rounds.

Both men went to their corners, in total ignorance of the fact that the timekeeper considered Smith to have been counted out. I never said "Ten!" never reached "Ten!" as the spectators and the contestants fully understood.

In America, I believe, they use a special watch for counting the seconds, but such a thing has never been done in this country. The referee does not stand with his watch in his hand. He merely counts ten at the rate of ten seconds as nearly as possible, conceivably giving the fallen man whatever fraction of difference there may be. On this occasion it was the timekeeper's opinion that fully ten seconds had elapsed. That may have been so, but it mattered nothing. The arrangement was that the men should go by my count, and it devolved upon me to count correctly.

Having refereed many hundreds of fights and always counted the same way, I have no misgivings whatever about the fairness of my count this time. If I took more than ten seconds to count nine—which, by the way, was not likely—then Smith had the benefit of it. I am also quite sure that he could have risen sooner than he did, had he not made up his mind not to get up sooner than was necessary. He did what all fighting men do in similar circumstances.

As it was, Smith gave some signs of grogginess on getting up, and undoubtedly welcomed the minute's rest between the fourth and the fifth rounds, which came immediately.

Carpentier from his corner looked on at his fallen foe without any feverish excitement, like a man who was saying to himself that sooner or later his enemy would go down for good.

Smith sprang forward for the fifth round like a giant refreshed, but strive as he might the Frenchman proved too clever for him, side-stepping and parrying his lunges with pantherine agility. That all this was galling to Smith could plainly be seen. Not once did his blows perceptibly hurt or disconcert Carpentier, and again the fifth round saw the Frenchman with a margin of points to his credit.

CARPENTIER AND GUNBOAT SMITH

Backers of Smith were now "hedging," as I was told afterwards.

Spectators as a whole were asking by what means Smith had acquired so great a reputation. On his showing that night he could not be given a place in the long list of great American heavy-weights of the past. Yet Gunboat Smith had a short time before beaten Sam Langford, one of the toughest and craftiest representatives of the coloured races. So, I suppose, one must say of Gunboat Smith that his performances are as unaccountable as his reputation.

The sixth round was sensational and eruptic. It produced the grandest row and squabble the sporting world has witnessed for many years. In the centre of the hubbub stood the referee as calmly and as self-possessed as a man who, being surrounded by a hornet's nest, knows that the wisest thing to do is to stand still and not hit back. I am not going to hit back now, for there is nothing to hit back about.

I did what I believed to be the right thing, and a man can always look the world in the face, enjoy his dinner, and sleep soundly when he knows that. On the whole, the preponderance of opinion from sportsmen of importance on both sides of the Atlantic supported my action. That is always gratifying to a referee, but at the same time it would not have mattered in the least degree to me if I had alienated the opinions of those whose judgment I value most, so long as I was thoroughly satisfied of the soundness and honesty of my decision.

I was in the ring and could see best. Every yard of proximity is important in such emergencies.

Things went on in the sixth round very much as usual, Smith palpably becoming desperate and Carpentier correspondingly confident.

The crisis arrived in a very simple manner. The Frenchman sent a terrific right hand over, and missing Smith, who cleverly dodged it, fell on his hands and knees. He then got up with one knee on the ground, his toes postured tightly like a runner starting in a sprint race.

It was then that Smith perpetrated the foul which ended the fight. It was unmistakably a foul blow. Take that from me, who was there within a few paces to see it.

The American swung his right hand at the man who was down, and hit him on the back of the head. It is no use discussing whether Smith intended to foul him or regretted having fouled him. The fact remains that he contravened the rules of the Ring by hitting his opponent when he was down.

M. Descamps immediately claimed a foul on behalf of Carpentier, and no other course remained open to me but to give Carpentier the fight.

Pandemonium broke loose. The audience unanimously cheered my decision, with the exception of Smith's manager, Mr James Buckley, who shouted, "Robbed! Put-up job!" adding, with questionable taste, hardly pardonable even in that heated

"Daily Mirror" Photo.

CARPENTIER AND GUNBOAT SMITH 41

moment, "How much, Mr Corri, did you have on Carpentier ? "

For that unsportsmanlike taunt he did not get what he deserved. I did not prosecute him for slander ; I never so much as thought about doing so. I scarcely paid any heed to his words. I left the incident for what it was worth, and that was very little. No manager in any fight that I have refereed among any class of boxing men ever behaved so excitedly and so badly as Mr James Buckley did on that occasion. I well know that Americans were ashamed of his conduct. On returning to his home on the other side, Gunboat Smith wrote me an extremely nice letter about the whole matter, which showed him to be a very good fellow indeed. Mr Buckley never apologized. Enough said.

If one or two of Smith's backers wanted to kill me ; the French people present wanted to kiss me. So there you are, and you can adjust the balance at your pleasure. It was contended that Descamps jumped into the ring before I had given my decision. That is not quite right. My mind was instantly made up that Carpentier could have the fight on the foul if he claimed it.

I turned my head aside for an instant to see whether the Frenchman was disposed to fight on. He evinced nothing but signs of great distress, and it was impossible for me to come to any other conclusion but that the foul blow had incapacitated him. It is true that Descamps got into the ring before I formally gave the fight to Carpentier, but not before I had made up my mind so to act if Carpentier and his manager claimed the foul.

For these reasons the presence of Descamps in the ring was of no consequence.

I said to Mr Buckley, Smith's manager, " You have had my decision." And so saying, I walked away. The M.C. announced my decision, and my duties were over.

Afterwards I told Mr Buckley that if anybody had been favoured (and assuredly nobody had) it was Smith, by my not giving the decision against him till I had looked round to Carpentier to ascertain whether he cared to go on. Had Carpentier showed fight, I should have let the fight proceed, because it was a good fight before a great assembly, for a great purse and for a great distinction.

I have not the gift of second sight. I could not see how much damage Carpentier had suffered by Smith's blow on the head. To all appearance, the Frenchman was badly injured, and in the little time at my disposal to judge of the extent of his injuries the impression that took hold of me was that he had not only been fouled, but felled.

Smith knew he had fouled him, and his gesture immediately afterwards indicated his regret for the expensive mistake he had made, though he described the blow as only a " flick."

I did not receive the blow, and cannot say how

CARPENTIER AND GUNBOAT SMITH

heavy or light Gunboat Smith's "flicks" fall. But I should think even a casual "flick" from the Gunboat, falling on the back of a man's head, would be apt to make an impression. So satisfied was I of Smith having fouled Carpentier, that I did not even start to count the Frenchman out.

While the sporting press of the world were discussing and freely criticizing the result of the fight in acres of hot print, Carpentier silently slipped away back to Paris to be loved and lionized like a national hero. The estimation in which he held Gunboat Smith was shown by the fact that he engaged Tom Kennedy, the great heavy-weight, who had fought Smith, to assist in his training. He had also Terry Keller, another American boxer, as one of his sparring partners.

Smith was equally careful about his preparations for Carpentier. In addition to Bob Armstrong, the ponderous nigger, his trainer, he had for sparring partners Kit Black and George Munro, the latter once the feather-weight champion of America, with whom he boxed to acquire quickness. Munro was very clever with the gloves. It was he who brought Kid Levene to England to fight Dick Burge for the light-weight championship of the world at the National Sporting Club. I have already mentioned Dick Burge as the promoter of the great Smith v. Carpentier fight, and he organized that splendid function perfectly. On the night of the contest people walked in a most leisurely manner to their seats. There was no rushing and no confusion whatever.

I remember Smith saying to me, " All Americans speak well of you, and I think you will be the right man in the right place as referee of the fight." He reminded me that I had previously refereed many of his countrymen, including Tommy Burns, Billy Papke, Jimmy Clabby, who subsequently became the middle-weight champion of the world, and Jimmy Britt.

Within a month of the Smith *v.* Carpentier contest I also refereed the fight between Freddy Welsh and Willie Ritchie, the latter being challenged by Welsh for the world's light-weight championship. The mention of Ritchie's name recalls a story that will make patriotic Englishmen smile.

He was going down to his training quarters at Brighton, and on the road they pulled up at the famous old Burford Bridge Hotel. The manager, after lunch, was showing them over the place, and said, " This was Nelson's room."

Ritchie replied cheerily, " Why! did Bat train here ? "

The hotel-keeper was thinking of England's national hero, and the pugilist of his namesake, Battling Nelson, the famous light-weight!

CHAPTER III

BOMBARDIER WELLS, WITH A WORD OR TWO ABOUT CARPENTIER

OF all the hundreds of heavy-weights I have known, Wells is one of the most remarkable characters, considered personally and socially. He is as docile as a big dog that disdains to emulate the yelping and yapping habits of smaller canines. It is like extracting a double tooth to try and draw him upon the subject of boxing. He fights with his fists and not with his tongue. No man was ever less of a swaggerer or bragger. Let him sit down with a chatty child on his knee, and he is at peace with all the world.

I have seen him in the stalls of a theatre of varieties at Southend, where he then lived, when one of the girl singers ingeniously worked his name into a topical song. He blushed scarlet, covered his face with his hands, and plainly wished that some trapdoor would open on a subterranean exit by means of which he could escape to the street. Sooner than have had the attention of an audience thus directed to him by a grimacing comedienne, Wells would have gladly forfeited the price of a dozen seats.

As everybody knows, Carpentier has long been the idol of France, and, I may add, the darling of Frenchwomen. To-day he is a national hero, and he deserves his laurels. He is without exception the Beau Brummel of boxing. In the ring or out of it, Carpentier is a dandy. There have been handsome boxers in my time, notably Jackson, who used to be compared to a bronze statue, and was generally spoken of as "Gentleman Jackson." He deserved the compliments that were showered upon him, though possibly his personal vanity and popularity overthrew him in the end. But Carpentier is the Adonis of the Ring.

On the occasion of Carpentier's fight with Wells at Ghent, a quarter of the audience was composed of women, and every blow of Wells as it fell upon his rival's body seemed to bring tears to the eyes of his fair worshippers. When ultimately the Frenchman brought down the English champion with a resounding body blow, the scene was one not soon to be forgotten. I and my compatriots were enormously despondent when Wells succumbed, but it was no small relief to our chagrin to behold the exuberant glee of the Frenchwomen, who swarmed to the ringside and lavished their kisses and caresses in a delirium of delight upon their handsome young hero.

I know Carpentier well. He possesses all the natural charm that characterizes the finished Frenchman. His manners are delightful, and might well excite anyone's envy; but these things do not comprise the character of Carpentier. There is in him as much of the bulldog tenacity and courage as any Briton ever possesses. He can be frightfully fierce, though in saying so I must not be thought to convey that he violates the traditions of the Ring. He fights fiercely, but he fights fairly, and never, so far as I have seen, subordinates his art to floundering violence. He is not quite Wells's equal as a boxer, though here again I must point out that his cleverness is very remarkable at critical junctures, while his hitting power at close quarters is astounding.

Shorter by inches, younger by years, lighter by many pounds, Carpentier is an opponent worthy of the respect of any man in the fighting line of to-day. All along I had my fears for Wells.

I have seen most champions that count: the thundering John L. Sullivan, the remarkable Fitzsimmons, the bearlike Jeffries, debonair Jem Corbett, the swaggering Johnson, the incomparable Jim Driscoll—all of them, I might say, with a little exaggeration. But not one of them has interested me in the same way as Carpentier; none has so fascinated me, none has so perplexed me, as the young Frenchman, who, I learn, though the war has cost him many thousands of pounds, is brimful of cheeriness and optimism and all the virtues that go to make a real man.

I am mindful of the danger—a common one, I would add—of overestimating the boxing qualities of Carpentier ; it is a danger that comes from the quiet of the fellow, his earnestness and naturalness. But that he touches greatness cannot be denied, neither can it be questioned that he has done more than any other boxer of recent times to bring about a better understanding and keener appreciation of boxing ; he has done much to give the sport its right and proper place in the scheme of things which we call life. This because, very much in the same way as he learned to box and fight as few could do, he has given to the game an atmosphere which until comparatively recent times it did not enjoy : he has given to boxing his personality. He has always been Carpentier, abundantly confident, grimly determined, and a man who took to the Ring as you and I would take to an everyday business.

It used to be said that a Frenchman could never be a great boxer because of temperamental reasons, because he was too volatile, too explosive. Carpentier has completely killed such a notion, for he has proved that in the ring at least he is a man of phlegm, tremendously matter-of-fact, a man with a clear-cut plan of campaign, and a man who, without any apparent effort, so applied the curb to his feelings that he suggested he could not be ruffled.

The only time I believe him to have been frightened and scared was when he was mobbed upon his arrival at Charing Cross for his fight with Gunboat Smith. He could not understand why he should be seized and squeezed and hugged. And he flew to his hotel.

If ever a man ran the risk of being spoiled and made balloon-headed, it was surely Carpentier. When he first met the ex-Bombardier Wells at Ghent, and, as you know, won in a most dramatic way, he was glad to take himself to his café near to the post-office. There I found him, with one of his eyes slightly blackened, sipping tea and eating cake. Outside of his room was a queue of expensively dressed ladies, most of them young and captivating, waiting to offer him bouquets of flowers. And when I told Carpentier that he was likely to be carried off, he just smiled, went on sipping tea, and waited patiently until he found an opportunity to run away.

The next time I saw him was when he was in training at Manitôt for his second fight with Wells. How he worked! how he trained! It did not matter that he had knocked the Englishman out at Ghent; he worked like a steam-engine, and with a method that was almost uncanny. He felt that at Ghent he had found a sure way to defeat Wells—that was to make a target of his body. And for hours on end in the improvised gymnasium at Manitôt did he punch away at a tightly stuffed bag. Now and then he would look round, and in a queer, amusing way would say in his best English: " Your Bombardier—see ? " And away he would go punching that bag, crouching the while, perfecting his in-fighting and seeing only in the bag the body of Wells.

The Mysterious Bombardier

I suppose no pugilist ever upset so many calculations as Billy Wells, once the champion English heavy-weight, who won his spurs, if ever a man did, by purely scientific fighting. I know Wells better perhaps than anybody, with the exception of his manager, Jem Maloney, and he has reversed my opinion of him more than once. It is about as hard to measure Wells as it is to measure one's own shadow. He is never twice the same. One day we prophesied great things for him, and were fairly up in the stirrups upon having discovered a brilliant White Hope ; the next day we shook our heads, and almost shook our fists at him. Was Billy downhearted ? No. He merely kept on smiling, and told us he would fulfil all our expectations some other day.

We have called him chicken-hearted, and we have seen him lion-hearted. We have said he lacked the punch, and we have seen him deliver it, until, baffled by his contradictory performances, we gave him up as a mystery. From first to last Wells believed in himself, apparently careless whether we believed in him or not. It was this trait in his character that always steadied my wavering faith in him.

The real trouble has been his inability to take punishment from the best of big fellows. On the other hand, there have been occasions when he has taken, as it seemed, no end of punishment, and then won on points, and even knocked his man out.

BOMBARDIER WELLS

To his great credit it must be said that Wells is amazingly clever at avoiding punishment once he has fairly got going. That is just the difficulty. On too many occasions he has displayed a dangerous tendency to hold an opponent too lightly at the start, and it makes one pause to think of a punch from Johnson or Langford landing on Wells's " weak spot " in an unguarded moment, where the fists of Carpentier took the wind from him on two occasions.

Quick as Billy's wits are, he has done lots of witless things, and disappointed his supporters by neglecting chances offered to him.

That Wells can hit, and hit very hard, goes without saying. He broke the jaw of the tough Irishman, Paddy Mahoney; and it was of Wells that Gunboat Smith said to me, pointing to his broken nose : " That guy did this, and if anybody can hit harder, I have never met him yet. When I fought Wells in America, he hammered me like a kicking horse. Things were going badly for me, when I let a loose one go, and landed on him at the back of the head somewhere, I do not know where. I only know that down went your English guy."

My friend Mr Seymour Hicks saw the fight between the Bombardier and Al Palzer in America, where he was then touring, and from the actor's account it was, in sporting slang, " a horse to a hen " on Wells. Mr Hicks was dumfounded when Palzer knocked him out. The audience was equally astonished, having been Wells to a man up to that moment.

They stood up at all parts of the building and shouted for him. The result was a staggering surprise—just such a surprise as Wells has given us all at different times. I shall have more to say about this fight later.

I was really instrumental in bringing Wells to the front, and it looked for a time as if I should have the pleasure of discovering in him a world-champion.

The late Major Best said to me one day: " We have found a most wonderful fellow, called Bombardier Wells, who has just come to England from India, where he won all the army honours as a heavyweight. I wish you could get him a ' job.' "

Naturally I was delighted to hear of the coming man, and lost no time in arranging an exhibition spar for him at Wells's Club.

He had to take small money in those days, and an occasional pound or two for a spar was very welcome to the Bombardier. It was decided to engage St George's Hall, on the suggestion of Mr Ernest Wells. The Bombardier's opponent was another bombardier of the name of Mills—a curious similarity of names these are. The same night Packy Macfarland had an exhibition spar with Eddie McGoorty, which was one of the finest displays I have ever seen. In after years McGoorty beat nearly everybody who came against him.

Wells made a very good show, giving me the idea that he might go a long way once he got rid of a lot of bad defects in his style, notably that long curving hook with his left hand, to which he unfortunately clung too long.

In Fenchurch Street Station one evening, where I had only a minute or two to wait for my train, a newspaper representative buttonholed me, and said:
" Mr Corri, I believe ? "
I said : " Yes, that's me."
" I have been sent down," said the newspaper man, " by my editor to ask you if there is any white man that has got any sort of a chance with Jack Johnson."

I replied : " There is a great big, good-looking, handsome boy called Bombardier Wells. I saw him box last night, and there is no knowing how he may turn out."

The newspaper man, with an eye to a thriller, made my words a trifle rosier. Next day the pictorial morning paper had a picture of Bombardier Wells and a story to the effect that Mr Corri had discovered a man who could beat Jack Johnson.

How near the mark or how wide of the mark the pressman was, I hardly know to this day. Anyhow, the fortunes of Bombardier Wells were unquestionably furthered by that quick station interview. The young pugilist's star was in the ascendant, and how brightly it shone thereafter everybody knows. That is years ago. Wells was then nearer twenty than thirty. He is now nearer thirty than twenty, and is not a fallen star yet.

Immediately music - hall managers turned their

attention to Wells, and gave him large sums to appear on the stage. They printed on the programmes under his name a legend like this : " The man Mr Eugene Corri thinks will beat Johnson." It was giving Wells something to live up to, and I must say that from that day he cut a very creditable figure in the boxing world, winning fight after fight in quick succession, doing all that he was asked to do excellently well, until he came into the company of the giants.

When both at the start of their careers, Wells and Carpentier trained together at the Elm Hotel, Leigh-on-Sea, in the lifetime of the late John Foreman, whose death at a comparatively early age was deeply regretted by boxing men all over the country.

Carpentier was then training as a light-weight to fight Young Josephs, and his manager asked Wells one night if he would spar with Carpentier. Wells agreed, and the spar developed into a red-hot one, during which the Frenchman had to take much more than he bargained for.

What happened that night bore fruit, I have always thought, in after years.

Carpentier's manager was very cross with Wells for the way in which he set about the French boy, and together they planned out a campaign to bide their time and take their revenge some other day.

I saw that revenge fulfilled when in after years Carpentier defeated Wells at Ghent and in London.

It is a singular fact that what Carpentier learned at the Elm Hotel was carefully borne in mind, and he never forgave Wells for putting a very nasty right across, which he did not at all like.

His manager, Descamps, took Wells's treatment very much to heart.

I remember seeing the two of them sitting over the fireplace discussing the Bombardier's action, and, though I was not supposed to hear what they said as they whispered to each other in French, I could easily see from their gestures and the anger on their faces that Carpentier was being shown by Descamps how to " get his own back " by knocking Wells out whenever they should meet in serious warfare.

The way Carpentier shaped over that fireplace, showing Descamps with his fists that he understood exactly how the thing could be done, was reproduced by him both at Ghent and at the National Sporting Club, London, when he defeated Wells in the most dramatic manner.

Some people pooh-pooh contests between men who have previously sparred together, as if these matches were apt to be " put-up jobs." This is a ridiculous argument, for it is always on the cards that the friendliest of sparring partners may become the deadliest of opponents.

In the case of Wells and Carpentier this was proved. Moir and Wells were also sparring partners, yet they fought two of the hardest contests, each defeating the other.

They did not fight a third time, though I believe that Gunner always wanted to settle the rubber with the Bombardier. He failed, however, to bring off a third fight, and I think it was just as well, as the difference in years, to say nothing else, was very considerably in Wells's favour.

Going back to earlier days, we find Wells knocking out Gunner McMurray at Shoeburyness Garrison, in the second round, with a skill that nonplussed his opponent.

Next he fought Corporal Johnson at Wonderland, and knocked him out before the fight had gone very far. His fame soon spread, and there came a man across Wells's path who was destined to give him a real " leg-up " in the boxing world ; and again I was the go-between.

Mr Hugh Macintosh, the great Australian promoter, came over to this country and made things " hum " in boxing circles. He came to me and asked who was the most likely fellow I knew of among the English heavy-weights. I told him that Wells was his man, good-looking, a real clean boxer, and becoming more popular every day as the boxing world was getting to know him.

The popularity of Wells has been remarkable all along his career, whether winning his fights or losing them. There is a mesmeric something or other about the Bombardier which makes the people like him personally.

In America, for example, he is as great a favourite as any one of their own men. Indeed, I doubt whether, were he to go to New York again, his reception would not equal that of Carpentier in London.

They have not seen anybody on the other side so clever with his hands and on his feet since the days of Corbett, and the Americans are very partial to scientific fighting. The bulk of their heavy-weights in recent years have been of the slogging order— Jeffries and the Gunboat in particular. None of them combined punching with science so much as Fitzsimmons, though even he depended largely on his punch.

Mr Macintosh jumped at Wells. "Send him to me," he said. I sent him, and Macintosh was the first man to raise Wells's fighting fee to three figures. Previously a ten-pound note was about the most he had had for a fight. The enterprising Australian neither asked what Wells was getting nor what he was worth. There was no quibbling. He simply straight away offered Wells a hundred pounds, win, lose, or draw, for three fights at the King's Hall, Westminster.

His opponents were Corporal Sunshine, Private Voyles, of the Irish Guards, and Seaman Parsons, who was then on the destroyer *Pathfinder*, that was blown up by the Germans early in the war. Fortunately for Parsons, one of his admirers had bought him out of the Navy, and so probably saved his life.

In Corporal Sunshine the Bombardier met a man of great cleverness, strength, and endurance. Wells always declared that that was the hardest fight he ever fought. I refereed the contest, and perhaps Wells was a trifle lucky in winning.

He told me afterwards that for two or three rounds he absolutely did not know what he was doing or how things were going, except that he felt in a very bad way himself and could see vaguely that Sunshine was no better off.

In those days Wells did not know how to use his feet properly. He was always hopping on his toes, more like a ballet-dancer than a boxer. Repeatedly Sunshine knocked him down, but he got up again like a great cat.

The Bombardier quickly improved out of all knowedge. " Sunshine gave me the greatest gruelling I ever got," said Wells afterwards, " and how I knocked him out I cannot tell. You must ask Mr Corri, the referee."

It was with a punch on the jaw that Wells knocked Sunshine out.

The next to confront Wells was that fine fighter, Private Voyles, of the Irish Guards. It was a terribly tough fight, and Wells was all but knocked out. Time saved him when he was hanging limp over the ropes, ghastly pale and gasping for wind, to all appearance a beaten man. But he recovered in the most marvellous way, and knocked Voyles out with one of the best punches on the body I have ever seen. It was a real beauty, quick as the flash of a sword, perfectly timed and dead sure. It took Voyles's seconds some time to get him round, and Wells, I remember, looked distinctly anxious, fearing he had damaged Voyles.

Seaman Parsons was pretty badly beaten by Wells, who hit him so hard and often that I fear he was never the same man again.

He boxed several times afterwards, but with indifferent success. Ultimately he became the Bombardier's sparring partner, and the poundings Wells gave him in the gymnasium, while training for his big fights, showed that at any rate Parsons could take a more than average amount of punishment.

The coming man practised many new punches on him, this being apparently all in the day's work. I never saw a sparring partner knocked about so much. The Bombardier literally bombarded the Seaman. With all his suavity and apparent diffidence, Wells can be as furious as a tiger, and he does not lack that spice of stingo, without which even the most scientific boxer cannot hope for highest honours.

The superficial observer judges Wells to be deficient in pluck and pugnacity. That is a mistake. Behind his exterior mildness there lurks in Wells's composition all the essentials of passion. His personal pride impresses those who study him closely, and very often he swings a blow at an opponent in a way that seems to say, " Take that, you presumptuous varlet ! How dare you come into the ring with me ? "

Having won his first three fights for Mr Macintosh, the latter took a fancy to Wells and gave him a

fight with Porky Flynn, Sam Langford's sparring partner. I rarely saw Wells box so brilliantly as on that occasion.
He boxed like an artist from beginning to end.
Not only myself, but everybody with a knowledge of boxing who sat at the ringside at Olympia that night, prophesied that here in this tall, debonair, curly-headed young man we had a champion indeed.

As a Coming Champion

Wells now got as many fights as he liked; and the best of all training quarters is the ring, where a man can measure himself against his challengers and ascertain his real worth. The ring also provides a test for a boxer's nerve; and however much a man trains, the gymnasium and the sparring partner cannot provide this.

The Bombardier had set his mind upon becoming a champion and girding his loins with the Lonsdale Belt. He came to England from India with a fine collection of cups, which included one that proclaimed him the most scientific boxer in the Indian Army. He has all these cups still. But they fell far short of satisfying his ambitions.

Gunner Moir and "Iron" Hague were the two men he had principally to reckon with. For a brief season Hague, the Mexborough giant, held the championship, which he won from Gunner Moir, the hero of a fierce battle with Tommy Burns, at

BOMBARDIER WELLS

the National Sporting Club—the only time Burns fought there.

Hague was a wonderfully game fellow with a terrible punch, of whom Langford said that he had never been hit so hard by anybody. The Mexborough man gave the nigger an eye-opener by knocking him down at the National Sporting Club in a fight which I refereed.

But Hague very soon tired of fighting in the front rank, to the great disappointment of his admirers, of whom I was one. Having won the championship, he practically retired on his laurels and gave up serious training.

When Wells fought Moir at Olympia he was "all over him," and people had actually left the building before the fight ended, feeling certain that Wells had won. But a fight is never over till it is finished, and there is many a slip in this as in other spheres.

Moir was as often on the floor as he was on his feet, but the strong fellow managed to keep on getting up until a chance came, when he landed a punch which nearly broke Wells in half, causing the Bombardier to measure his length on the floor, a beaten man.

They fought again at the Canterbury Music Hall, and Wells returned the compliment by first of all out-boxing Moir, and then knocking him out. These two fights unquestionably prove that Moir's day was done—he had had a very creditable innings—and Wells's day had dawned.

Boxers come and go in a long procession, and if championship honours are to be won, it must be on the sunny side of thirty. Instances are rare to the contrary. Moir had won for himself a place on the roll of championship honours, and he had now to be content with the prefix " ex."

With his championship honours upon him, Wells now sought new fields to conquer on the other side of the Atlantic, where his fame had preceded him.

The brightest white star in the American firmament at the time was Gunboat Smith, who had got a decision against Sam Langford at Boston, the latter's own town—a fact which accentuated the importance of Smith's victory.

The Bombardier's reputation was not heightened by his American performances, though he greatly delighted the Americans by his scientific displays. His three principal fights were with Smith, Palzer, and Kennedy.

Twice he was defeated and once he won.

There is a remarkable similarity between his fights with Smith and Palzer, each of whom knocked him out in the second round, after he had made them look clumsy in the extreme.

Palzer, a big fellow of the Slavin type, with a right-hand punch, scored practically no points till he landed the blow which made points of no account. The contrast between the two fighters suggested the well-worn comparison of a bull and a panther. It was a contest in which physical strength triumphed over science, early in the contest, to the disappointment of all who witnessed it.

Wells fought his opponent to a standstill, and gave the American public a never-to-be-forgotten taste of his hitting powers. With a magnificent right-hand punch the tall, slim-looking Bombardier lifted Palzer clean off his feet, as if a ram had butted him. He fell forward and practically stood on his head some seconds.

Nobody thought he would get up in time, but he did, and stayed on to the end of the first round, receiving a terrible hiding.

The audience was delirious with joy at what they had seen and what they were likely to see from Wells, but as fate would have it, they were destined to see very little more.

It was Al Palzer's turn next. In the second round he landed one of his best on Wells, who went down all of a heap and remained down, to the great astonishment of everybody. People were not so much surprised at Wells not getting up in time as at the fact that so clever a boxer should have let himself be knocked out so soon.

It is peculiarly true of the American people that they have no use for a beaten boxer, turning their backs on him and looking for a man with a series of victories to his credit.

They had seen Wells beaten, but they did not treat him in this way. The spirit of sportsmanship rose to the occasion, and they made a notable exception of the brilliant Bombardier, to whom they gave as great a reception, when he bowed to them, after being pulled round, as to the man who had beaten him. The papers lauded Wells to the skies, and he was fêted everywhere. They liked him for his clean style of boxing, and bated nothing in their admiration of him.

This was still true when Gunboat Smith beat him in very much the same way as Palzer had done. Again the audience was roused to the utmost enthusiasm by Wells's wonderful showing in the first round. He had them all at fever-heat by the way in which he outclassed Smith as a boxer. To Smith's credit be it said that he never crowed over his victory; for it is due to the Gunboat to say that, with all his bluffing mannerism, he was at heart quite a good fellow and a real sportsman. I have already told how he knocked Wells out.

The Bombardier always wanted to have another go at Smith, and he may yet. The war was indirectly responsible for the Gunboat's return to America after his fight with Carpentier in London, the arrangements for a contest with Young Ahearn having been unavoidably postponed till such time as the British public should recover from the shock of the terrible carnage on the Continent, and were again in the mood for witnessing their favourite sport.

Wells's only victory in America was over Tom Kennedy at Madison Square Gardens, New York.

Kennedy was a fighter more after Wells's stamp, and the spectators saw two clever fellows pitted against each other.

Here again the superiority of Wells as a boxer was abundantly demonstrated. The Press gave columns to him the next day, and he was generally lionized by the public.

A famous boxer used to say that he could gauge his standing with people by the amount of attention paid to him in the streets by little boys. Wells was followed everywhere, and had his name shouted to him with congratulations wherever he appeared in public. Boxers are easily identified, and none easier than Wells, the overtopping blonde.

His visit to America was a brief one, and he was soon back in London, preparing to meet all comers. Within the period of a few months he fought Bandsman Blake, Bandsman Rice, Colin Bell the Australian, and Georges Carpentier.

At this time he introduced a novelty to his training system in the form of golf and rowing, with a marked preference for golf. When the weather was suitable, and also when it was far from ideal, he could have been seen on the golf-course at Mitcham, often playing alone, eagerly studying the fascinating game, which my friends have long recommended to me without results.

He told an interviewer that it was his ambition one day to become a golf champion as well as a boxing champion; but I believe he afterwards modified that ambition upon discovering that to excel at the royal and ancient game required more attention than he could afford to give it.

They told me at Rochford that he drove a ball three hundred yards when playing his first round. It was not a straight ball, however, but left him as far to go to reach the green as if he had not hit it at all! I know nothing about golf, and am indebted for this information to a golfing acquaintance who played with Wells on that occasion.

Bandsman Rice took Wells all the twenty rounds at the Stadium, Liverpool, and I fancied that Wells was very used up in that bout. It was a close thing. Some sporting writers went so far as to differ from the referee who gave the decision to Wells.

His fight with Bandsman Blake took place at the Palladium Theatre of Varieties, London, and in the first two rounds the musical boxer had slightly the better of things. Blake gave a good deal of weight away, being only two or three pounds over the middle-weight standard. In the third round Wells caught him a nasty punch with the right hand, which left Blake very groggy. In the fourth round the Bombardier finished the Bandsman.

All Wells's fights since his return from America were of minor importance compared with his return match with Georges Carpentier.

It was this contest to which the public were looking forward with intense interest, impatiently counting the days till the night of the fight, which will go down in

BOMBARDIER WELLS

the annals of istiana as unique. It would have broken the heart of a less buoyant boxer than Wells to make such a sorry show.

Gunner Moir said he could never have lifted his head up again had Wells's fate happened to him, but the Bombardier was philosophical enough to take what the gods meted out to him and go on with his training, in the firm determination to redeem himself.

The story of this fight is told in a sentence, but there are some incidents, before and after it, which seem worth relating, in conjunction with the fight between the same two men at Ghent a year or so previous.

Wells was decidedly unlucky to have lost the fight in Belgium. I saw both contests, and talked with the two men a good deal at the time. I remember meeting Wells on the morning before the fight, strolling in the streets of Ghent with his trainer Jem Maloney, and I remarked how well he looked. He said he was feeling first-rate. One always expects boxing men to say this sort of thing on such occasions.

I also saw Carpentier sitting outside a café, drinking coffee. He had his overcoat on, and the collar turned up. It was in the morning, and apparently he had just returned from a motor ride. His appearance did not impress me at all well. I thought he almost looked dejected, sitting there hunched up within the folds of his greatcoat. He speaks English about as well as I speak French, and that made conversation practically impossible. We only exchanged a few words, which exhausted his store of English and mine of French.

I went down to his training quarters at Manitôt. There I found him surrounded by a great staff of sparring partners, amongst whom was Demlen, the celebrated Belgian welter-weight. No man ever worker harder in the gymnasium than Carpentier.

I was struck by the evident delight he took in his work. He is a great walker, but he does not walk like a professional walker, who has no eyes for the scenery and no thought for the society in which he moves. To Carpentier walking is not a task, but a very real joy, such as one experiences rambling in the country on a spring morning or an autumn afternoon. It is an article of faith with him that little good comes of anything unless a man throws his whole heart and soul into it and extracts a thrill of pleasure from it.

The French boy is also fond of a gun, and said to be a very good shot. On returning from a walk and having a good rub down, he goes up into the hills to shoot rabbits, as a relaxation, during which boxing affairs are suspended.

A rich French admirer placed his château at Carpentier's disposal, and there he lived, studied and petted in every shape and form.

I lunched with Carpentier, and afterwards we had music, vocal and instrumental. I never saw a happier training camp in my life. It might have been a party of well-to-do holiday-makers. Not a soul spoke of boxing.

Mr Bettinson was one of the party, and as he had to go back to Paris by an early train, he was anxious that Carpentier should go into the gymnasium and do a little work rather earlier than the appointed hour, for the boxer's entire day is most methodically mapped out. Descamps, his manager, said to Mr Bettinson, with a gesture of regret : " Not for the King of England." Carpentier's daily programme permitted of no alterations even to oblige the manager of the National Sporting Club.

The violinist of the party was Carpentier's mascot, an independent little French gentleman of delightfully simple manners. He worshipped Carpentier, and was ready to do anything to oblige or amuse the national hero. I remember a funny incident in the gymnasium. They got the mascot to referee a bout between two of the big sparring partners. We laughed uproariously as these fellows contrived to fall into a clinch, while the puny referee perspired in his attempts to separate them. " Break ! " he would shout in his piping voice, that being possibly all the technical English he knew. Carpentier's face was a picture of uncontrollable mirth as the mascot endeavoured to enforce his judicial authority.

For our entertainment the mascot stripped to the waist to do some shadow boxing. His display was the funniest thing imaginable, but laugh as we might, it never for a moment occurred to him that it was his simplicity that amused us.

One of the party also introduced a bit of byplay

in the shape of a practical joke which I have seen played among parlour games in England at Christmas. I think it was Mr James White who suggested it. The game was called " Finding a threepenny piece." A black felt hat was dented, and a quantity of soot from the chimney was rubbed into it.

The mascot immediately undertook to lead off. A threepenny piece was placed in the hat, and he was challenged to remove it with his teeth. Valiantly did the little fellow struggle, meanwhile, of course, thoroughly blacking his face unawares. We laughed till our sides ached, and Carpentier almost went into hysterics.

The unsuspecting mascot wondered what we were laughing at, and every time he asked us we laughed the louder, as his face became more and more comical-looking. Afterwards he came out into the open air with his face still sooty, as no one troubled to tell him what had happened.

Carpentier's mascot died a little while ago, and the boxer must have felt his loss very much, because he invariably had him with him at his fights. It was almost a case of Prince and jester.

The Two Fights

Surely Carpentier must have the very best manager in the world in the person of Descamps, who waits upon him hand and foot, never allowing him to be molested or troubled about anything whatever. The boxer is very fond of a game of cards, and Descamps turns this weakness to good account.

On the eve of a big fight he will get together some friends to start a game of cards. Carpentier soon becomes so engrossed that he forgets all about time, and possibly plays on till four or five in the morning. Descamps is delighted. He puts his pet to sleep, and places a guard outside his bedroom door, or even does sentry duty there himself.

To anyone who approaches that door he will say: " No, no; Carpentier asleep." The boxer will get up late in the afternoon, and practically go straight from " bath and breakfast " into the ring.

Descamps trains on intelligent lines. How many managers would care to let their candidate for championship honours, or a purse of thousands of pounds, play cards all the night before a fight ?

Maitrot, who was killed in the war, after winning a commission and several decorations, refereed the fight at Ghent, and he refereed it from the inside of the ring. This is the rule practically everywhere, except at the National Sporting Club. My own view has always been that the inside of the ring is the proper place for the referee, so that he may miss nothing. The practice prevails in America, Australia, France, and in all the provincial towns of England wherever boxing contests are held.

It has always been the custom at the National Sporting Club for the referee to judge the contest from outside the ring, and I suppose something can be said for it. My opinion is, however, that there are many little things about a fight, especially about in-fighting, which necessitate the referee being in the position to view the contest closely and from all sides. Boxers have broad backs, and you cannot see through them.

With this digression I come to the fight at Ghent. Carpentier came into the ring with all the buoyancy of a boy. He looked very pretty in his white shorts, striped with pale blue down the sides, but a sorry picture he presented on retiring to his corner after the first round.

Women were weeping all over the audience to see their idol so terribly disfigured. Wells had visited his handsome face with a succession of stinging jabs, and his features were besmeared with, as the old writers used to say, a "plenteous supply of home-brewed claret." Not a few of the women present had come from London with their sporting husbands.

That Wells would win nobody for a moment doubted. But Wells did not win, and I leave you to imagine how sick the Bombardier must have felt when he realized how very stupidly he lost.

In the second round things went worse than ever for Carpentier. He was at one time hanging helplessly over the ropes, with the back of his head to the audience, utterly unable to defend himself.

Wells slung a hard right-hand at him, and Carpentier cleverly slipped it with his head, showing that his wits remained though his strength was gone,

BOMBARDIER WELLS

and he fell into a clinch to which he stuck as long as the referee would permit. The end of the round came, and the minute's interval made a new man of him.

The third round saw the amazing young fellow on the aggressive; and in the fourth round he was all over Wells, finally knocking him out.

Women fluttered into the ring to kiss him. His admirers carried him shoulder high. Wells looked very downcast and fairly used up. Carpentier had finished him with exactly the same punch that he used at the National Sporting Club about a year afterwards, when they met for the second time.

After the fight I said to Wells: "When you had him hanging over the ropes, why did you not hit him underneath?"

Wells replied: "I never thought about it." If ever a man wished he'd done anything which he'd left undone, Wells was that man at that moment.

Wells's blunder raises a curious point. It was with a right-hand punch that he knocked Carpentier over the ropes, and it was with a right-hand punch that he tried to finish him.

Boxers invariably do this. If they find that they have hurt a man with a particular punch, they try to do the same thing immediately afterwards. It is a strange example of self-imitation, and is usually a mistake, because if the man has been badly hurt, his attitude undergoes a distinct change from that which he assumed when the damaging blow was delivered. In such a juncture the winning man should have all his wits about him to adapt the next blow to the altered situation.

I have already said a good deal about the fight between Wells and Carpentier at the National Sporting Club—the fight which lasted just long enough for a well-known member, who had come in a second or two late, to place his opera-hat in a leisurely way under the seat, and sit up again to find that the fight was over.

On the night of the contest, Carpentier arrived at the National Sporting Club first. He went up to his dressing-room, which is situated on a floor they call " Old London," on account of the way in which the place is done up.

An hour before he was going to fight for the championship of Europe, this extraordinary young fellow was so composed that he started pitching pennies at a line drawn on the floor with his manager, Descamps, and he played as keenly as if that was the only business on his mind. Carpentier has cultivated concentration to an astonishing degree.

Wells arrived during the game, accompanied by his manager and several followers. Carpentier looked up a second and said : " Ah, Beely, are you well ? " " Yes," said Wells. " Good," said Carpentier, as he went on playing at the game.

Those of us who know Wells can imagine the impression produced upon his sensitive nature by such an uncommon incident. The thought of Carpentier's coolness could not fail to disturb the Bombardier, as he reflected upon the self-assurance of his opponent, who could play at pitching pennies a few minutes before going into the ring to meet him.

Putting two and two together—remembering Wells's manifestations of nervousness—who can say how much that incident had to do with his collapse? I am quite sure that it was no case of scientific bluff on the part of Descamps and Carpentier. They had no idea whatever of parading their composure before Wells, but simply played at pitching pennies to while away the time and reserve all their nervous energy till it was required. There is a great object-lesson for all boxers here.

Carpentier came into the ring first, and Wells kept him waiting a long time. This, however, had no effect on Carpentier. He merely turned to the gentlemen sitting in the front seats, members of the aristocracy mostly, and appeared to be interested in their fine clothes. He told his manager afterwards, who asked him what interested him then, that it was "the gentlemen's buttons."

I did not like the look of Wells that night. Nobody did. Certainly he stripped to perfection, but his manners and the look of his eyes did not inspire confidence.

Carpentier rushed right into him and punched him in the jaw. Wells put up his hands and Carpentier punched him in the stomach. Wells lowered his hands, and Carpentier then visited his jaw. Once more Wells raised his hands, and still once more,

76 REFEREEING 1,000 FIGHTS

and several times more Carpentier hit him in the stomach, using both hands in a succession of rapid blows, literally hammering the big man to the floor.

We can all be wise after the event, but it is still true that we could see Wells to be suffering from a species of stage-fright. I can find no better term.

He bowed to the great reception accorded to him like a man who hardly knew what he was doing, or where he was.

The moment the gong sounded he nervously gulped a mouthful of water, and stood in one position as if his feet were frozen to the floor. This was most unlike him. As a rule he makes the most of the ring. Carpentier did not fail to note the nervousness of Wells, you may be sure. He is a very quick-thinking boy.

When it was all over Wells stepped forward to the ringside, and, holding up both hands in a pitiable, apologetic attitude, said : " Gentlemen, I have done my best." He was honest, but we knew he had done his worst. Carpentier, having shaken hands with him, left the ring, a double conqueror.

On the following Saturday Wells played football for a charity on the Chelsea ground, before many thousands of his countrymen. He told me that he felt more nervous on appearing on that football ground than he did when he entered the ring to fight Carpentier. He wondered how the multitude would receive him. He had not long to wonder. The moment he appeared the crowd rose as one man and cheered the unfortunate pugilist. I believe he scored several goals on that occasion.

Nothing amused him so much as when, sitting at his dining-room window on the morning after the fight, with his first-born on his knee, a passing milkman, noticing him, sang out : " Who were you with last night ? " The Bombardier very nearly dropped the baby.

Mysterious Billy Wells !

Colin Bell and Wells

Great interest was aroused when a match was fixed between Colin Bell and Wells, to take place at Olympia. Bell had been very little heard of when he arrived in this country from Australia. But there was a great flourish of trumpets over his showing against Joe Jeannette, the wonderful black boxer, who was given a verdict against Bell, after twenty rounds, while the audience, or a great part of the audience, voted Bell the winner.

I only mention this to indicate that the fight was well contested, and any man who could take Jeannette twenty rounds, as Bell did, would naturally appeal to the fancy of boxing men. Joe Jeannette had long proved himself to be a front-ranker.

Mr Hugh Macintosh has always said that Jeannette would beat Langford in a contest to a finish. He had fought Sam McVea, one of the longest and closest fights on record, and knocked him out. All these things considered, therefore, Bell's performance raised him very high in the opinion of some of the best authorities.

Wells witnessed that fight, and came away with the opinion, which he freely expressed, that he thought he could defeat Bell in six rounds. As a matter of fact he did better than this, knocking him out in the fourth round.

Colin Bell was just about the nicest fighting man you could meet in a month of travels. He had absolutely no swank or bombast, and though making no parade of modesty, he yet never, when speaking of Wells, went further than to say that he hoped to make a good fight of it, and that the best man would win ; as undoubtedly the best man did. Bell was too slow for Wells.

The burly Australian Bushman was never fit in this country, and complained of nose and ear trouble all the time he was training at the Hampstead Gymnasium. I believe he underwent an operation shortly after the fight.

I do not mention these things to minimize Wells's victory, nor even to explain Bell's defeat, because I believe Wells could always beat Bell.

I refereed the fight, and Bell always said that the blow which finished him landed on his bad ear. But from my position inside the ring I knew that it was a punch on the point which put him out.

There was great rejoicing on the part of the general public that the Bombardier had regained his form, as it was believed that in beating Bell he had done something more than ordinary.

The Australian came with the reputation of never having been knocked out, and it was even said that he had among his credentials a victory over Sam Langford. What a lot of fighting men there are who lay claim to this distinction! It appears that when a man can get it said of him that he has survived ten or a dozen rounds with Langford, or, better still, knocked him down, his claim to respect is assured.

I wonder whether the nigger ever fights with his tongue in his cheek, charitably making reputations for white opponents. Be that as it may, I cannot think of any white man who would have been capable of standing up to Langford, when he was over here and in his prime, very much longer than Langford would have been disposed to let him.

CHAPTER IV

ROBERT FITZSIMMONS

I KNOW a white man who might have beaten Jackson, both being in their prime. I do not refer to Mace, Sullivan, Mitchell, Slavin, Corbett, or Jeffries. I allude to Robert Fitzsimmons, who held simultaneously the middle-weight and heavy-weight championships. Fitzsimmons was nearer forty than thirty when he won the heavy-weight championship from Corbett, who was then at his best.

Corbett was an accomplished boxer, about as hard to hit as a shadow. He was everywhere at once, except where his opponent's blows fell. No man ever preserved his features free of damage through so many hard-fought battles as "Pompadour Jim." It is Corbett's pardonable boast that his face emerged unblemished from fifteen years of hard fighting.

Fitzsimmons could take punishment until his opponent exhausted himself administering it. Then came his opportunity for that conclusive solar-plexus punch of his, which passed into a saying with the man in the street, so that London larrikins could have been seen experimenting with it on the kerbstones.

What a fighter Fitzsimmons was! I saw James Corbett and him meet in a London hotel years after their battle at Carson City, when Corbett was winning on points till the blacksmith delivered that terrible solar-plexus blow which doubled up the one-time bank clerk like a half-shut knife, wresting the championship from a man who a year or two previously had plucked the laurels from the brow of the incomparable John L. Sullivan, who immortalized the saying : " Never strike a man called Sullivan."

They talked of this fight, and still, at a long distance of miles and years, differed about the precise nature of the knock-out blow. But their friendliness was an object-lesson in sportsmanship. No prominent boxer in the whole history of the noble art was ever a churl. His great encounters necessarily preclude the possibility of his character deteriorating to such mean levels.

Fitz and Jim laughed and joked like old schoolboys who never had an enmity of any sort whatever. At my request, they sprang to their feet and reproduced the last scene of their championship fight. They squared up to each other in the corridor of that hotel like two old tigers that still had the fire of the jungle in their eyes—Corbett still straight as a mast ; Fitz nearly ten years his senior, but capable a year later of surviving fifteen rounds against Bill Lang in Australia.

I have always regretted not taking a snapshot of the impromptu exhibition in that London hotel. An admirer opened a magnum of champagne in commemoration of the meeting of these master boxers of a bygone day. I noticed that neither Corbett nor Fitz took more than a sip of the wine. Their fighting days were done, but the manly art had deepened the love of life and good health. They were both better without alcohol, and so they gave it a miss— " side-stepped " it, in the phrase of the ring.

Corbett smoked the choicest of cigars. I should say he was almost a chain-smoker, like the late Mark Twain, who lit one cigar with the burning bitter end of another. Jim confessed that the weed was his master. In vain he struggled to break with it, but had given up the contest as hopeless. " I am the bond-slave of the best of all possible masters," he used to say.

Fitz feared cigars ; one a day spoiled his sleep. Discovering this, he resolutely reasoned : " Are not seven hours' sound sleep better than one comforting cigar ? " He plumped for sleep, and I know where there is at this moment a gold cigar-case, given to him by an admirer, which he apologetically declined lest it should lure him back to the old enemy.

How many of us could do that ?

In the early days of my refereeing career I was timekeeper for B. J. Angle, and no one could ever have had a better trainer in the judicial department of boxing than I had. Mr Angle was the greatest referee England has had for a generation. Very seldom did an audience resent his rule, and the fighting men themselves were equally satisfied with the justice of his decisions.

Referees are, in a sense, both born and made. You must have something in common with the men whose work you are watching. You must have a good nerve and a quick eye ; and, having made up your mind regarding the relative merits of the fighters, there must be no dubiety about your decision or lack of courage in declaring your verdict. That is the great thing, and it comes from experience. You soon learn to be firm and fair alike in conducting the fight, so as to eliminate everything contrary to the rules, and in estimating the points in each man's favour.

These you must quickly seize upon as they are presented. Every audience is crammed with critics who form their opinion as the bout continues, and do not shrink from letting the referee have the benefit of their views upon his ruling and final award, whether it is just or otherwise. They will hurl epithets at you with even more vigour than happens on the football field.

You must have no ears for the partisans in the audience, but all eyes for the participants in the ring. Often the referee wishes he had eyes all round his head, like Argus, the hundred-eyed shepherd of ancient mythology. The referee takes almost as much out of himself as the fighting men. I believe in a referee watching a fight from the inside of the ring. I have already remarked that this is not done at the National Sporting Club, but it is done practically everywhere else. Personally, I always take up my position within the ropes, because it is so easy for one to miss points—good points and bad points—at a distance.

My system of awarding points is to make five the highest possible for any one round. It often happens that the difference in the total of points scored by two men is very slight, and I have not infrequently declared a draw when this happened. For example, if a champion were fractionally beaten by a challenger, I might decide, having regard to all that was at stake for the champion, to make the fight a draw until he should be more decisively defeated. My marking card is for my own exclusive guidance, and in the case of a long, closely contested fight, decisions are not so easily given as may seem to the uninitiated. In many of the rounds the points gained by the combatants may be indicated in fractions, and then, I suppose, my Stock Exchange experience in dealing with " differences " proves useful.

I only referee fights under the National Sporting Club rules. It is not generally known that one of these rules empowers the referee to give the verdict in favour of a man although he may be actually counted out. The National Sporting Club takes no official cognisance of the knock-out, though, of course, we are all aware that a knock-out blow is deemed to be conclusive. Still, suppose a case like this : One man has been winning handsomely all along the line to the twentieth round, in a specified twenty-round contest.

In the last round, let it be argued that the man who has figured so splendidly is suddenly knocked down by a chance blow and counted out. The rules of the National Sporting Club would, in such a case as that, justify a referee in giving the fight to the man who had so conspicuously proved his superiority on points.

Here, for example, is the sort of card that would place the referee in an awkward dilemma :

POINTS

Bombardier Wells, 95 points (at the end of the nineteenth round).
Gunboat Smith, 60 points (at the end of the nineteenth round).

Let the card also show Wells knocked out by Smith in the twentieth round. If the fight were, in that case, as it very possibly would be, given to Smith, that would mean that the knock-out blow was more than equal to thirty-five points, and that the man who had been palpably losing throughout the whole fight was yet declared the winner.

The first essential in a referee is a practical knowledge of boxing. He must be something of a fighter himself, though not, of course, in a professional capacity. The knock-out blow requires little refereeing ; the counting of ten seconds decides that, always providing that the man who delivered the decisive blow did so fairly and squarely. I know no sport or game, call it what you like, in which the quality of fair play comes so vitally into force. The reason is obvious. To "hit below the belt" is a phrase that has crept into everyday speech. When it is applied in any walk of life, in work or play, we mean to convey that a man has done something unworthy of an Englishman and a white man.

Only in a battle-royal among niggers is everything and anything permitted, short of using a pole-axe or a coke-hammer. A "battle-royal" is a contest among a dozen, or it may be a score, of black men who are thrown together into a sort of cockpit. The nigger who survives the lot is the conqueror. Every man's fist is against every other man's, and any two or three, or more, may be against any one of the number. That, of course, is black and barbarous. Such black pugilists as Peter Jackson, Jack Johnson, and Sam Langford all distinguished themselves in these terrible battles-royal.

I have very many times seen a man an easy winner on points up to the moment when a telling blow from his opponent vanquished him and discounted all the points that stood to his credit. It is like a fight between a collie and a bulldog. The nimble collie registers many points to the good for a time, but the bulldog takes his punishment with stubborn *sang-froid*, and waits his chance. In the end it comes, and woe betide the collie when the teeth of the bulldog close upon his throat.

CHAPTER V

WILLIE RITCHIE AND FREDDY WELSH

THE language of sporting parlance is generally more expressive than any amount of fine writing. It illumines a story like striking a match in the dark. Freddy Welsh had for years been pursuing Willie Ritchie all up and down America to "get him into the ring" with him, as the saying goes. His persistency, after a long series of annoying disappointments, was rewarded with a match which took place at Olympia, London. It remained to be seen whether Ritchie could "side-step" Welsh in the ring as he had "side-stepped" him out of it. I am afraid it was his turn to be "side-stepped" now. I had the honour and pleasure of refereeing the twenty-round contest, which "went all the way," resulting in a win on points for Welsh.

The audience got full value for their money, in striking contrast to the short fight between Carpentier and Gunboat Smith, and the still shorter fight between Wells and Carpentier, some time previously. Ritchie and Welsh were well matched, both being, in their class, as game and clever as could be desired.

I had never seen Ritchie until I met him at the Piccadilly Hotel, London, where Mr C. B. Cochran, the promoter of the fight, had invited me to meet him. I found him to be a swarthy, very nice-looking young fellow of pleasing manners. He said he had heard lots about me in America, and for that reason had stood out for me to referee the contest.

"There is only one thing, Mr Corri, which I want to ask you," said Ritchie, "and I should like to settle it right here. It is about the bandages."

In America, I may say, they use all sorts of bandages, some not unlike "knuckle-dusters."

"I do not want," said Ritchie, "to keep everybody waiting on the night of the contest, while we are squabbling about what we are going to wear. I should be perfectly satisfied to wear the bandages they use at the National Sporting Club, and let it go at that. Are we going to put the bandages on in the ring, or are we going to come in with them on?"

I replied that as a rule boxers put the bandages on before getting into the ring, and that Dr Matthews, the celebrated bone-setter, who has done more for boxers' hands and wrestlers' knees than anybody in the world, would be there to superintend the fitting-on of the bandages.

Ritchie replied : "Well, he is good enough for me if you say so."

When Bombardier Wells fought Carpentier at the National Sporting Club, he kept the young Frenchman waiting and wearying while he had his bandages

WILLIE RITCHIE AND FREDDY WELSH

adjusted. Bandages are worn to protect the pugilist's hands, which are to him what tools are to a workman. Usually the seconds on either side see the bandages put on, to satisfy themselves that everything is right. Perhaps, if anything, bandages brace a punch up. A man with weak hands would always rather box with his knuckles protected ; for once a boxer's knuckles are gone, his occupation has gone also.

Welsh had no questions to ask, and readily agreed to abide by anything Ritchie wanted. He attended the reception given to Ritchie at the Piccadilly Hotel, where, as stated, I first met the young American boxer. The two contestants—one the champion of America, and the other the champion of England—were to fight for the higher honour of the light-weight championship of the world. They chatted together freely, and impressed all beholders with their self-assurance and easy manners, each apparently confident of winning, though neither making any prophecies. I talked to both of them together with regard to the bandages, and other preliminaries, neither putting any difficulties in the way.

Welsh's manager, Mr Harry Pollock, was also present, and altogether it was a very merry and harmonious gathering. What Mr C. B. Cochran is on this side of the Atlantic, Mr Harry Pollock is on the other—top-dog in the fight-promoting business. You might describe Cochran as the Pollock of England, and similarly speak of Pollock as the Cochran of America.

All the negotiations went off excellently, but a funny thing happened to me which showed that I was still a long way from being known by headmark to everybody. On the day of the weighing-in at Olympia I happened to lunch at Wells's Club, Bond Street. Of course, everybody was talking about the fight. There were a number of gentlemen present who said they would like to run down to Olympia and see the weighing-in, which took place at the regulation hour of two o'clock. Lord Clonmell said : " I will send through for my car," and an officer of the Scots Guards said he would do likewise. We all drove down to Olympia without delay, and found an enormous crowd waiting outside.

I knocked at the door, which was opened a few inches. I called out : " My name is Corri. I am refereeing the fight to-night. I want to come in." The stern and dutiful doorkeeper replied : " That is all right."

I thought it was ; but it wasn't.

The doorkeeper went on : " We've had several Corris down here to-day. Eight o'clock, you."

After keeping me standing there not in the best of humours for fifteen to twenty minutes, repeating, " My name is Corri," in my most imperious manner, I had to give in, as the fellow behind the door would not even condescend to take my card. My friends did not see the weighing-in, but they hugely enjoyed the joke at my expense, remarking that I was the finest thing in referees they had ever met. Eventually a higher authority than the doorkeeper admitted us, but not before the weighing-in was all over.

In America matches are usually made "Weigh-in at the ringside."

Ritchie trained at Brighton, and I went down there to see him, taking with me my two boys, Toodles and Micky, both of whom are well known among the young boxers of England. We saw Ritchie at his work at the Albion Hotel, which is kept by the brother of Mr Harry Preston, whose excellent qualities as a host are known to all sportsmen and newspaper men. Mr Harry Preston formed one of the party, and at his suggestion Toodles and Micky put on the gloves to Ritchie, and needless to say, knocked out the champion of the world with ridiculous ease! Ritchie entertained the hotel guests, amongst whom were many women, with an exhibition of shadow-boxing and skipping on the roof-garden.

For the benefit of those who may not have seen shadow-boxing, I may say briefly that there is no shadow in it. The boxer neither fights with his own shadow nor anybody else's shadow actually. He imagines himself to be engaged with an opponent of great cleverness, and endeavours to meet every attack of the illusory combatant, behaving very much as if he were engaged in an actual contest. People who saw Ritchie shadow-boxing that day and saw him afterwards fighting Welsh, would have readily guessed that the opponent he had in his mind's eye while shadow-boxing was Freddy Welsh. Had pictures been taken at the Albion Hotel and compared with pictures taken subsequently at Olympia, a striking resemblance would have been very noticeable.

Shadow-boxing is exceedingly hard work, as the pugilist spends his blows in the air with nothing to stop them. Any footballer will tell you that to lunge at a ball and miss it is almost like throwing one's leg away. So the shadow-boxer, though he is receiving no blows, is yet vigorously engaged delivering them. I think it was Bombardier Wells who once said that he had to develop so much concentration while shadow-boxing that he could almost fancy he saw his imaginary opponent in the flesh before him.

Ritchie stripped finely, every ounce and inch an athlete, much stronger-looking than Welsh, and I could see then that a great treat was in store for the vast audience at Olympia. It is quite a common thing in these days for referees to do as I did on that occasion by going to see Ritchie. The fact that I was to referee the forthcoming fight had nothing whatever to do with the case. I hope it will always be true of British referees that they are incapable of partiality. Welsh trained at Porthcawl in Wales, and that was too far for me to go. But for this, I should certainly have gone to see him also.

If I were to compare Willie Ritchie with Freddy Welsh in a general sort of way, taking no account of what either one or the other has done in the boxing world, I should say that there is more of the born fighter about the American than the Welshman.

Though training and hard study of their art must have gone far to bring them both to the high position they have attained, I should say there is more of the self-made boxer about Welsh than there is about Ritchie.

Welsh could not be correctly described as a strong young fellow—strong, that is to say, in the sense of being endowed with great natural strength. To him boxing is an engrossing science, and he has been ready and willing at all times to sacrifice everything to it, denying himself every luxury that threatened danger to his physique ; and I am given to understand that for many years he has been wealthy enough to regale himself with most of the alleged good things of the world.

Brainy to a remarkable degree, Freddy Welsh is a first-class example to young men all over the world in the splendid religion of body-worship. His method of training is very largely original, though, to be sure, he has not neglected to read and inwardly digest the styles and systems of all the greatest exponents of boxing. To lovers of physical fitness it is a pure delight to see Freddy Welsh at his exercises. That wonderful will-power of his has literally built his body to the pattern carefully prepared for its development.

The unintelligent observer might suspect Freddy of being something of a crank. But nothing could be further from the truth, unless by a " crank " is meant one who knows what is good for him and has the moral courage to defy existing conventions and carry out his own doctrines. A teetotaller, a non-smoker, a vegetarian ! So he is spoken of as being, and so he practically is. But not altogether. He can and does on occasions drink wine, smoke tobacco, and eat meat. But none of these things has any real part in his system of living. If you had him, say, at your house as a guest, you may be sure that he would obtrude none of his prejudices upon your notice. You may be also sure that he would give you the real pleasure of seeing a guest thoroughly enjoy his host's entertainment. There would be no excesses, except the one grand excess of social enjoyment. He might drink one glass of wine or two glasses of wine, smoke one cigarette or two cigarettes, and eat meat as heartily as anybody else. It would be exactly the same if you were a vegetarian (for Freddy revels in fruits and vegetables), a teetotaller and a non-smoker. He would neither miss the wine, the weed, nor the meat. Nor would he enjoy himself one whit the less, but possibly more.

There you have, in my opinion, an ideal young fellow, and what British parent would not like to see his boys possessed of such fine control over their appetites on reaching manhood ? I have dwelt at some length upon Welsh, his method of training, and his mode of life, because I know no young man in the boxing world or out of it for whose personal character I have a greater admiration.

We come now to the fight. You can picture the

WILLIE RITCHIE AND FREDDY WELSH

scene for yourselves : Olympia packed to its limits with sportsmen from all parts and of all grades. Americans in strong force, eager to see their clever countryman do them honour ; perfervid Welshmen singing, as only Welshmen can, in fine harmony, that great song of the Principality, " Land of our Fathers," and all the world waiting to learn the result and read detailed accounts of the contest, round for round. That is not how I should describe it in my capacity as referee, though I could still at this day reproduce it from beginning to end, so vividly did it impress me on that night, and so clearly does it come before me now as I sit with half-shut eyes in a sort of reverie as a spectator, shorn of my official responsibilities.

First of all, the great event was led up to by the preliminary of getting some notable boxers to step upon the stage and bow their acknowledgments. These included Young Ahearn, who went to America ; Tony Ross, the Italian-American heavy-weight ; Coffey, the Irish Giant ; and Bombardier Wells, the English heavy-weight champion. Each had his meed of applause, but Wells got most. There was also some for me when I jumped into the ring, carrying in my hands the gloves to present to the fighters.

Ritchie and Welsh hopped into the ring together, and the audience no doubt began to compare notes, intensely admiring both the young fellows. I took the contestants aside and went through the formality of reminding them what they might do and what they must not do—"read the Riot Act" to them, so to speak.

Immediately they touched gloves, swung into position, and went at it full tilt. From the start Welsh showed how clever he was.

It was said that Ritchie was a slow starter, and that he boxed six rounds with one of his sparring partners just before the fight, so as to liven him up. If that was so, it did not seem to have the desired effect, as Welsh was "all over him" in the first round. Ritchie was relying, as he did throughout, on his celebrated right-hand punch, with which he beat all his opponents—excepting the same "Freddy the Great," who beat him. In no one of the twenty rounds was there a wide margin in Welsh's favour. As a matter of fact, three of the rounds were Ritchie's, but only three. Seventeen rounds, with a fraction of advantage in each of them, made a substantial aggregate for Welsh, and it is just possible that he eased off a little during the three rounds in which Ritchie held the upper hand.

It was a beautiful fight on scientific lines from start to finish, and I rarely experienced less trouble in refereeing any contest. I had explained to the men that they were to break away the moment I might tell them to do so, as I was not there to do any weight-lifting. They obeyed me to the letter. The merest tap on the shoulder was always enough to separate them when they clinched. Anyone seeing the fight on the cinema screens might have thought

that I had to push them apart, but the quick eye of the camera was not quick enough to show how easily these separations were effected. The men actually jumped asunder, so ready were they to obey my instructions. It was very different in the fight between Smith and Carpentier, when I had to exert not a little strength on more than one occasion. I remember Smith's manager calling out to me, " Throw them apart," as if I were a " strong man " put in the ring to exhibit my powers. To Welsh and Ritchie I had only to say the words, " Break away," or " Take that arm away," when the thing was done.

Somewhere about midway in the fight, Welsh got a taste of Ritchie's right punch, and I believe it shook him up a bit. It was a finely delivered blow, but Welsh saw it coming and managed to avoid its full weight. Perhaps it was just as well for him that he did, for I imagine that if it had properly got there it might have finished the fight.

Each man knew all about the other's style of fighting, and knew exactly what to expect if either got too much of his own way. It must have been sickening to Ritchie to see his punches miss, not once or twice, but many times, by the margin of a foot. The audience laughed as the tricky Welsh boy glided out of his opponent's way, and even Ritchie himself smiled in an uphill sort of manner, till he positively hesitated about trying his punch for fear of bringing ridicule upon himself by missing. That great punch of his had played havoc with a succession of opponents in America, but here he was fighting a pugilistic genius who could hit "and get away" with accuracy and agility that bamboozled Ritchie. Having received one punch, and that only in moderate measure, Welsh promised himself never to receive another, and faithfully stuck to his resolution.

The fault about Ritchie's fighting was his habit of "telephoning" his punches. Welsh fixed his eyes, or one of his eyes (the other being aggressively engaged) upon Ritchie's right hand, and he could see the American gradually drawing that right hand further back by degrees until it reached the distance at which it flew forward as if released by a spring, when his opponent dodged it with ease.

As the contest wore on its long way, Welsh knew that, bar a knock-out, he could win, and he took no chances, keeping himself up to concert pitch with wonderful endurance to the end. He also knew—and this might have depressed anybody else—that he could not hope to knock Ritchie out. It is a singular fact that Freddy Welsh owes none of his great reputation to knock-out blows, but almost entirely to the fact that he has baffled all his opponents in their attempts to knock him out, while he went merrily on adding to the sum of his points. It is a great fame for a young man to have, and affords a splendid example of the supremacy of science.

I am not insinuating that Ritchie is devoid of science. Far from it; but, like Johnny Summers, knowing that he possesses very exceptional hitting power, he has naturally yielded to the temptation of cultivating his punch and trusting to it for success. Welsh's tactics negatived that punch, and his "in-and-out" cleverness won him the fight. Ritchie tried his hardest, hoping against hope, and fighting as pluckily as ever man fought to "get there," but failed.

I never tire of analysing Welsh's methods. He had brought to perfection the great trick of keeping his elbows well in, stopping Ritchie's left hand with his right and Ritchie's right hand with his left, thus being always "inside his man." Very few boxers know how to stop a right-hand punch. Mr Bettinson, manager of the National Sporting Club, when in his boxing prime, was one of the first men who ever showed us how to do this. Jack Johnson knows all about it, and when he brings those mighty forearms of his to bear, pushing his opponent's arms to one side or the other, it is almost enough to knock a man off his balance, if not off his feet. Carpentier is another who knows how to do this, and I fancy he has acquired it by studying Johnson. It is a style that opens up the way to most effective lifting upper-cuts with the right hand right from the hips, the calves, and the very foot. It is quite a new punch, and the boxer who has it must always be a dangerous foe. Bombardier Wells lacks this punch, trusting to his long curving left, which has served him well in many bouts, but possibly accounts for his twofold defeat at the hands of Carpentier's in-fighting cleverness, inasmuch as a long wide punch leaves the body unprotected.

Welsh in his class, Johnson and Carpentier in their classes, stand out unequalled in their day.

When Wells defeated Porky Flynn at Olympia, I turned to Sam Langford, who was standing near me, and asked him what he thought of Wells. With a chortle the humorous nigger said : " Waal, he is very tawl ; he has a great left hand ; he is verra clever on his feet, but I think I'll draw the colour line." Did anybody ever say a cleverer thing than that in all the acres of print that have appeared upon the colour question ?

I saw neither Welsh nor Ritchie after the fight, but I read somewhere that Ritchie was disappointed, as he expected, at the worse, that I should have given a draw. He said, or the interviewer said for him, that in America he would have been declared the winner on the ground that he fought on the aggressive all the time, whereas Welsh never really came at him. Whether Ritchie said those things or not, he certainly knows, as all fighting men know, that points are not given for mere aggressive fighting. To rush at a man without hitting him, but rather to be hit by him, is not the way to win a fight. Ritchie certainly chased Welsh round for round, but—oh no, Willie !—it would never do to award points for blows that meet the air. You are a magnificent fellow, strong as a young lion, and more than a match for any light-weight of your day, excepting Freddy

Welsh, to be beaten by whom, as you were, in the manner you were, need not greatly dim the lustre of your fame.

You won a fine purse—five thousand pounds, if I am not mistaken, having stipulated for this amount, win, lose, or draw. Freddy Welsh did not put very much in his pocket over the fight, but he gratified the ambition of his life by winning the light-weight championship of the world and the coveted Lonsdale Belt—an honour which you will be the last man to grudge him. It may come your own way yet. The Americans at Olympia that night were satisfied that Welsh had won handsomely. Some of them retired before the finish, remarking that only a knock-out blow could give the verdict to Ritchie.

One of them said to me afterwards: " Welsh is a wizard, as hard to hit as a snipe. We cannot teach him anything on the other side about in-fighting. I lost more money on that fight than any other man in the house, but, Mr Corri, I'm satisfied with your decision."

CHAPTER VI

MATT WELLS, SERGEANT BASHAM, AND JOHNNY SUMMERS

NOT the least interesting of the many contests I have refereed was the bout between Sergeant Johnny Basham and Matt Wells. Both are boxers of interesting personality. Basham, who won his championship when he was a sergeant in the Royal Welsh Fusiliers, is a most modest and unassuming young fellow, an accredited champion and yet devoid of any suggestion of side. Incidentally he is quite one of the best welter-weight boxers I have ever seen; but more of that later.

He won his Lonsdale Belt from that good boxer and likeable fellow, Johnny Summers, who, in an unguarded moment, left himself wide open and encountered one of the most decisive knock-out punches I ever saw.

Instead of going for what the boxers call the "easy money," Basham took on Matt Wells, a dangerous opponent at his weight for any man in the world. There were several aspects of this match which were specially interesting. In the first place, it was staged in the beautiful London Opera House, that remarkable building in Kingsway which, since it arose at the bidding of Mr Oscar Hammerstein, who was going to show London what Grand Opera really meant, has passed through so many vicissitudes.

And then, this was the first big spectacular contest arranged by an outside promoter that had taken place since the outbreak of the war, nearly eight months before.

It was a model contest in more ways than one, and certainly it was so from the point of view of the referee. Once or twice I had to warn Basham not to hold, but they were trivial offences on each occasion, and for the most part the man boxed a genuinely clean and honest battle.

And what a contrast they made, physically and in styles of boxing! Basham is a clean-limbed young fellow, lithe and graceful in all his movements, and carrying the graceful poise and balance of a symmetrically proportioned athlete. Over in the other corner was Wells, a squat figure of a man, inches shorter than Basham, and yet carrying very clear evidence of unusual strength. He has always been a most interesting figure since the days he came to the front while a member of the Lynn Boxing Club, but always he has had to contend against his lack of inches.

It followed that with such a build he would have to rely to a not inconsiderable degree upon his ability to "fight" his opponent, subordinating nearly everything else to a plan for getting to close quarters and pummelling away with half-arm punches. That is all very well if your opponent is not sufficiently clever to stall you off; if he is sufficiently clever, then it is odds on the boxer against the "fighter" every time. But do not run away with the idea that I am classing Wells as just a wear-and-tear "fighter"; he can box, and box exceedingly well. I merely mean that his strength, taken in conjunction with his shortness of stature, has made a policy of getting in toe to toe the right policy for him on most occasions.

Matt Wells has the real fighting face. He is one of the sunniest-tempered fellows in the world, and yet he can look grim enough when the game of boxing is on hand. And he does not look at all an easy man to knock out, with his barrel of a chest and his wonderfully fine development of neck and shoulders. Some years ago, when he won the light-weight championship, he was very speedy, and there were those who contended that after he had grown into a welter-weight his added poundage had meant a loss of speed. But I am bound to say I saw no indication of this in his memorable bout with Basham. I think if he had a fault, it was that at times he was just a wee bit over-cautious. I expected to see just a little more "devil" in his boxing, especially towards the close, when his hope of victory lay in a knock-out. At the same time, in fairness to Wells, it should be added that, as Basham boxed that night, any opponent who knew his business would have thought twice before taking risks.

MATT WELLS, BASHAM, AND SUMMERS

I had been prepared for something good from Basham, but not quite so good as we got. In attack and in defence he was brilliant, and to the expert lover of the game his display was a sheer delight. He could never afford to take things at all easily, and yet he always appeared to be boxing with genuine confidence. Wells tried his very hardest to get close to his opponent and hammer away at the body, but the splendidly effective cover up of Basham was a perpetual stumbling-block in his way. There was no suggestion of the American cover in Basham's methods — it was just most admirable defensive boxing.

His left leads were as good in their way as anything I have seen; timing and judgment of distance were alike consistently excellent. There may not have been a great deal of sting behind the glove, but it was impressively clever boxing.

Another phase of Basham's boxing that I admired very much was his ringcraft and generalship. He has not had a particularly long or varied experience of the game, but apparently he has little to learn in head-work. More than once he was in really tight corners, but always he was extremely sure of himself and never in the slightest degree flustered or haphazard. It was as well for him that he was not, for Wells was a most worrying and persistent opponent, who was always working for a chance to send along a decisive punch.

Upon three occasions during the contest he shook

Basham, but the soldier was never once in a condition of anything approaching distress. He got just in front on points and was apparently satisfied to keep there, eschewing anything in the least risky, and carefully avoiding boxing that was merely flashy and spectacular. There were several periods when he reminded me strongly of Jim Driscoll. There was not, perhaps, the sense of quiet mastery that used to be conveyed by the Welsh wonder, but there was much else that called to mind the late champion feather-weight of the world.

After a few rounds Matt Wells began to wear a rather anxious look, a dull flush overspreading his features. But the fact that he was not exactly happy made him no less dangerous an opponent. Times out of number he would rush in, attempting to beat down Basham's defence, but nearly always the same thing happened : the soldier, with a bit of smart defence, would take the honours, and then a moment later would indulge in strenuous attack on his own account.

A lot of the boxing must have been above the heads of the crowd, and yet all present seemed to appreciate the fact that they were watching something more than a little out of the common, and at regular moments there were bursts of applause, Wells, perhaps, being a slight favourite, although the house was a very fair one.

He had started, by the way, a 7 to 4 on favourite, odds which, in my opinion, were never justified, for

Basham was no 7 to 4 against chance with any opponent in the world. Towards the close there were some lively attempts to "hedge" on the part of the men who had laid the odds. As the last round or two passed, I heard stray remarks wondering "if Corri will call it a draw." There were those present who believed that if there was a winner it was Basham, but that Wells had done just enough to merit a draw. For myself, I was thoroughly convinced that the soldier was "well there." Wells was always knocking at the door, and this fact may have conveyed to some the impression that he was doing all the work. But how often did the door open ? That was what one had to consider.

I am told that Wells was chagrined at the decision, but I venture to believe that his own immediate supporters recognized the fact that, good and clever though their man fought, his opponent went just one better. I left the London Opera House that night wondering where there was a better welter-weight than this Welsh sergeant.

In ordinary clothes you would never take Basham for a champion, but once "in action" the merest novice could see that here was a man of real class. I am not overfond of prophecy, but if Basham's future is not very bright I shall be surprised indeed. I believe he is a very careful young fellow in all things, and there would seem no reason why he should not have many years of prominent activity in the Ring.

Let me finish with a little story about the personal side of Johnny Basham. When the stakes were paid over the next day, Matt Wells's backer urged a return match over twenty rounds. Basham smiled, and said: "Your turn will come, Matt, and I'll always be glad to box such a good sport, but my next engagement is all fixed up." Matt stared in surprise. "Who is your opponent?" he queried. "Kaiser Bill," jerked out Basham, and proceeded with his cigarette.

How Sergeant Basham triumphed over Johnny Summers

Johnny Summers missed the chance of a lifetime at the National Sporting Club on the night of 14th December 1914, in those bitter war days when the British lion was shaking his mane and showing his fangs to avenge the ghastly barbarity of the German Navy in slaughtering women and children by the bombardment on a misty morning of the unprotected towns of Scarborough and Whitby and the meagrely fortified Hartlepools. These weekly Club nights helped to relieve the racking strain of war.

Sergeant Basham had come up from the camp of his regiment, the West Kent, to cover himself with glory, decorate himself with the Lonsdale Welter-Weight Championship Belt, and win the substantial annuity of £1 a week for life at the age of fifty—something like an "old-age pension"! Basham was twenty-seven, so that the pension was still a long way off.

How old is fifty to a young man nearing thirty! Yet how young is fifty to a man who reaches it in sound health after a youth carefully preserved as Basham's has been! An actuarial friend of mine calculated that in Basham's case the pound a week for life was about equal to £500 down. It will be handy enough when it comes.

The N.S.C. had never previously given a purse like it. Basham won it on his merits, and Summers lost it through mistaken ring-craft. Science deserved it, and the soldier proved the more scientific boxer.

Everybody was sorry for Summers, who had won the Belt twice before, and had only to win it that night to make it his own. Among those who have won Lonsdale Belts outright at their particular weights are Bombardier Wells, Jim Driscoll, Digger Stanley, Tancy Lee, and Freddy Welsh. These Belts are really the blue ribbons of the Ring, and bear the names of all winners of one or two contests, while the man who takes a Belt home for good is in the happy position of a conqueror who may read on his trophy the names of all who have gone one-third or two-thirds of the way before him.

The hope was freely expressed that Summers might yet win it a third time before advancing years let younger men gain the upper hand of him.

"He cannot spare many Summers now," said a

member who was old enough to know better. Not guilty, my lord!

I fancied Basham from the first, though I had seen much more of Summers before the fight, as he trained at Shoeburyness, and I frequently saw him down there. He boxed much with the soldiers, and seemed to find amusement in letting the biggest and best of them punch his jaw as they pleased. No doubt it was pleasant to discover that his head sat so firmly on his short, thick neck that none of them could drive it back, punching their hardest. Johnny believed that nobody in England could knock him out, Sergeant Basham included. Many of the Shoeburyness soldiers were more powerful than he, and so Summers made the misleading deduction that he could safely offer his "point" to Basham in the same way. He forgot, as fighters will, that an ounce of applied science is worth a stone of misapplied strength. Therein lies the true nobility of the art we all love.

There was an extraordinary amount of money laid on that fight. I was told that one member of the Club had £300 on Summers—a lot of money in those hard times. I never saw Summers box better than he boxed that night. Time and again he made Basham miss him, not by inches, but by feet. In the opinion of every capable judge, he ought to have won. But in the end he surprised and disappointed us all. The unexpected happens so often in boxing that a backer is never out of the wood till the men are out of the ring.

MATT WELLS, BASHAM, AND SUMMERS

In the first two rounds Summers was seen at his best, and that is saying much. In the second round, with a beautiful left to the body and a right to the jaw, he had Basham undoubtedly in great trouble. It was only by wonderful cleverness that Basham stayed to the end of the round. We cheered him heartily, recognizing his resourcefulness and skill in manœuvring out of tight places.

Summers was underestimating him, and anything might happen. The way in which Basham made use of the ring space—walking about, getting into a clinch, and generally fiddling this way and that, keeping his senses clear so as to avoid punishment—made it very plain that here was a man far above the average, a man with a brain quick and steady to cope with emergencies.

The fight was a joy to watch, except, perhaps, for the man who had £300 on Summers. It never looked a certainty for the champion. Basham had proved his ability to keep out of the way of Summers, cheating the fighter of the chance he was playing for. The man who can do this is always the man for my money.

From this point on nothing could have been finer than the judgment Basham displayed. He boxed like one of the class craftsmen. With perilous persistency Summers took all the risks, regardless of punishment, thinking himself punch-proof. He would take anything Basham had to give, if only he could land one of his own smashing blows.

It is the oldest error of the Ring. Careless cocksureness is really a tactic of the tyro, and it surprised me to see an old and experienced man like Summers indulging in it. I don't suppose I ever saw any boxer push to such extremes the bad policy of tempting his opponent to hit when and where he liked.

"Does Johnny think he is immortal?" whispered a member near me. "Basham has not hit anything like his hardest yet, as you will see presently."

He was right! Summers thought Basham had gone all out, and that was just the impression Basham wanted to give him. It was a battle of wits, and very soon Summers was at his wits' end, for the enemy was anticipating his plans and upsetting them. Summers thought he could not be knocked out. His record to some extent warranted this confidence, but every dog has its day and every man his down. It came to Summers when Basham, seizing one of Johnny's invitations, let fly a punch he had reserved till the right moment came. Summers fell and slept through the count.

No man in that audience had ever seen Summers prostrated in that manner before. He had himself to blame, though Basham's performance must not be belittled in so saying.

Talking to Mr Bettinson after the fight, Basham said : " It was part of my game not to hit him hard with the right hand, because I did not want to let him know that I had a right. He fell into the trap which I laid for him, and pushed his jaw out purposely to be hit. Then I let one go with all the strength in my body. It took effect and knocked him down. He got up again in a very groggy state, and I immediately sent out another right-hander to the jaw, which knocked him down, this time not to get up again."

Basham was also an easy winner on points.

So ended one of the most interesting fights seen at the National Sporting Club during the War, and while it lasted it was a most exciting bout. It was a case of the fighter beaten by the boxer—a thing that more often happens than not, and cannot happen too often for the good of the Ring.

Both men were trained to the hour and fit to fight for a kingdom. The sympathies of the majority were with Summers, who had done more boxing than any man of his day. He had travelled from one end of the world to the other, freely issuing and accepting challenges in Australia and America. To have won this fight would have nicely capped his career, bringing him possession of the Lonsdale Belt and that not inconsiderable pension of a pound a week for life at fifty.

Wise after the event, Summers said: "I thought I had got Basham. I did not think he had a punch. I took too many risks. We live and learn, but I ought to have learned long ago not to go so far out of my way to look for trouble."

Basham was now well into the limelight, and men who had not fancied him "looked up his form."

They found that in Australia he had beaten McCormick, who had twice beaten Summers " down under," and a still greater proof of his quality was a victory over Young Ahearn at the Stadium, Liverpool. A real champion—dark, with a strong, clean-shaven face— Basham carried his well-won honours with quiet satisfaction, like a man who knew that he was just beginning to prove his worth.

It is a singular fact that I have been a sort of Jonah to Johnny Summers, inasmuch as he has never won a fight with me as referee. He did not win his next fight with Sergeant Basham at the Stadium, Liverpool, where it was left to me to give a decision on points in Basham's favour. I did not referee their fight at the National Sporting Club, and I do not suppose that my presence in the audience could by any stretch of superstition be taken still further to prove that I was Johnny's Jonah.

Of all the boxing men I have met, I am quite sure that none of them has been so great a favourite of mine as Johnny Summers. This fact has made it positively painful to me to keep on refereeing his defeats. Of course, a referee of any sort can never be influenced by his personal likes or dislikes. Nevertheless, it is a fact that nothing would give me greater pleasure or relief than to be able to declare Johnny Summers a winner—a pleasure which becomes more remote as the years go by. Once boxing men fall into the habit of suffering a succession of defeats, it is a hard thing for them—especially around the

MATT WELLS, BASHAM, AND SUMMERS 115

thirties—to retrieve their misfortunes. No class of sportsmen become " old 'uns " so early in life as pugilists.

The second fight between Basham and Summers took place soon after their first contest ; and it was very evident that both of them were determined to benefit by what they had so recently learned of each other. They seemed to me to be overcareful, as if each knew by experience that he had a tough job in hand. When it came to in-fighting, Summers had the best of it ; and when it came to boxing— absolute boxing—Basham shone supreme. They went the whole fifteen rounds, which was hardly what one would have expected after Basham's previous display at the National Sporting Club, taking account also of the fact that Summers invariably relies upon the knock-out for a win.

Both men were enormously popular with the Liverpool audience, and the Stadium was so well filled that you could not have got another walking-stick in. Basham had made his name in Liverpool, where nearly all his principal fights had been fought. Liverpool, by the way, has for years been making a bold bid for the distinction of being the greatest boxing town in England. I do not even put London before it in the matter of enthusiasm. For example, the gloves with which Summers and Basham fought were sold after the contest for thirty-five guineas, and a penny programme, bearing the signatures of Summers, Basham, and myself, fetched thirty shillings.

I suppose this money would be handed over to some of the war funds.

The fight itself need be described only in a general way. In the last round it looked as though my verdict might not be required, as the soldier shook Summers up very badly and gave many the impression that he was going to repeat the knock-out of their first fight. Basham is without exception the hardest fighter I have ever seen. He never seems to spare himself and never seems to tire himself. On the call of " Time ! " after each round, he rushes at his man, coming up with him before he has well left his corner. It is the same in the later as well as the earlier stages of the fight, and anyone coming into the audience as Basham left his corner for the fifteenth round might have imagined it was the first round, so energetic was his attack, leading off with his left hand according to his invariable habit. Though Basham won the fight, the margin of points was not a wide one. It was not a " walk-over " for him. No man ever " walked over " Johnny Summers. The decision was a popular one—popular in the sense that the audience concurred in it, not in the sense that Basham was the more popular man. There was not a single " Boo ! " when I announced my decision.

When I spoke to Summers afterwards I found him perfectly satisfied and very nice about his defeat, though he could not refrain from remarking : " Mr Corri, you have refereed me three times, and on each occasion I have lost. It is most extraordinary that I cannot win when you are refereeing."

I agreed, and Summers quickly added: " Still, there is no referee I would sooner have."

That was very courteous of Johnny, but it left me wondering whether the undoubted strain of superstition in his character might have hampered him in any way. I hope not, and hardly think so.

CHAPTER VII

WILDE THE WIZARD

WAS there ever a bantam-weight, feather-weight, or a boxer of any weight like Jimmy Wilde, of Wales ? Absolutely never—in my time, at any rate. Wells, Welsh, and Wilde—the least of these is the greatest of these. Wilde strikes all the lot of us almost dumb with amazement. We have to resort to exclamations in speaking of his boxing. Analyse him we cannot. His lightning speed, his perfectly timed blows, his gliding foot-work, and the manner in which those long, pipe-shank arms of his drive his opponents back reeling and blowing, or cause them to measure their length on the floor, baffle expert and layman alike. Surely science was never brought to such perfection as in his case. Brute force he has absolutely none, not an ounce or the fraction of an ounce, yet he hits as hard as if his thin arms were steel rods. So hard do his blows fall that he has several times broken his right hand on an opponent's body and been compelled to finish a fight, and win it, practically doing all the work with his left hand.

This most wonderful of all wonderful boxers is only a trifle more than seven stone, fully dressed. Up to

WILDE THE WIZARD

the moment of writing he has, I think, fought about eighty fights, winning them all but two, one of which was his defeat at the hands of Tancy Lee, the Scotsman, and the other was a draw. He has fifty-two knock-outs to his credit, the rest of his victories being secured on points. Yet almost every time he has been giving away lots of weight, sometimes as much as one and a half stone.

I witnessed his contest at the National Sporting Club with Young Symmonds, of Plymouth, who had recently defeated Percy Jones, the holder of Lord Lonsdale's Champion Belt. He boxed Jones at "catch-weights" — which in sporting terminology means any weight—and knocked him out.

The majority of the members of the National Sporting Club thought it would be impossible for any six-stone boy to give away weight in such proportion, but nevertheless Wilde accomplished it in the most convincing manner.

Early in the fight Symmonds hit Wilde undoubtedly very low, giving rise to cries from the crowd for disqualification. The referee, however, did not agree with the audience, and Wilde, who had set his teeth together, obviously suffering acute pain, went on to fight the whole of the fifteen rounds and win easily on points. What is still more remarkable about this fight was that Wilde, in the second round, fractured a bone in his right hand, so that from that point on his left hand got all the work to do. The pluck of the young fellow was magnificent. No " Stoic " or " Spartan " could have endured pain more heroically. We could see Wilde trying to conceal from the notice of his opponent that his right hand had been done up. But the way in which he nursed it left none of us in any doubt, and even Symmonds must have surmised what was the matter.

Those who have not seen Wilde fight should lose no time in doing so, if they wish to experience the delight of seeing a perfect human machine in motion, a born fighter whom no amount of training could have produced. Nature has cast Jimmy Wilde in a mould of her own, and the oldest follower of boxing will tell you that he stands alone, almost as a freak of fisticuffs. Bearing in mind his weight and the fact that he is fairly tall, you can understand how extremely thin and wiry he is. Small-faced and very pale, his quick eyes sparkling like jewels in his head, Wilde seems to be able to adjust his distances as exactly as a trombone player slides his instrument about to produce notes and half-notes at will. I can compare his arms to nothing else than long clay pipes, and it passes my comprehension how he can deliver blows that make strong men quiver, banging their heads back as if he would break their necks.

His judging of distances is beyond all praise, and his foot-work is the right sort of foot-work. He does not hop about on his toes like a kangaroo, but slithers on the soles of his feet in the style of a plantigrade. Quick as a wild cat, he drags his feet this way and that like a bear, and can strike with his paws just

WILDE THE WIZARD

about as hard. The only man whose foot-work resembles that of Wilde is Sam Langford, who never by any chance jumps an inch off the floor. The obvious advantage of fighting in this way is that the boxer can better keep his balance and delivers his blows with his feet flatly planted on the ground. When his opponent misses Wilde, as he generally does, by a fraction of an inch, Wilde advances suddenly and lands a hot return. He measures the distance to his man as precisely as he measures his distance off his man.

Rarely, if ever, does he train for any fight in the systematic manner. He keeps fit rather than gets fit ; having no ounces of weight to spare, he has no occasion to train off. A careful-living, natural young fellow, with a gift of boxing as surely as ever poet had the gift of musing, Wilde is ready at all times for all comers in his own class or a class above it. Jim Driscoll is his great model, if a natural fighter like this can be said to have any model. They are both sons of the Principality, plucky little Wales, which has given to the world some of the finest boxers of the past or the present.

If you were to make a record of the number of blows delivered by the ordinary run of boxers at the empty air in course of a fifteen-round or twenty-round fight, the total would run well into three figures. Not so in the case of Jimmy Wilde. This cool and collected master of the fine art of timing a blow hardly ever lets a punch go that does not land where he means it to land, or near it. An American who sat beside me was so carried away by Wilde's boxing that he said : " Why, in the States they would go raving mad over this boy. What a pity he is not bigger ! " Bombardier Wells put his hands to the sides of his head in sheer bewilderment, and kept on exclaiming, " What a marvel ! "

Wilde's modesty is as notable as his science. He hardly ever talks of boxing, and, like many other good boxers, he is extremely reticent about his abilities or performances. When Tancy Lee, the Scottish boxer, beat Percy Jones, Wilde turned to a friend sitting near, and said, " Ah ! I must fight Lee and get our own back for Wales." He did not boast of his ability to do so, but calmly expressed his intention of trying, in the firm belief that he could win. Wilde is a married man with sons, I am told, to whom he should have to give away a stone or two of weight. Think of him as a jockey, and you will gather some idea of his appearance. Then think of a jockey being able to acquit himself as Wilde can in a twenty-four-feet ring. This mode of reasoning will somewhat help you to form a mental picture of the Welsh phenomenon ; but when you come to the point of accounting for the dash and devil that is in Wilde, you will, I fear, find yourself as much in the fog as I am, and will arrive at the conclusion that it is hopeless to attempt to explain the achievements of a man who is not like other men.

If ever the term " genius " could be applied to

a boxer, then Jimmy Wilde is the boxer who best deserves it.

TANCY LEE, THE SCOT

To the rude school of caravan life Tancy Lee owed his training for the Ring, in which he quickly won his spurs. After his fight with Jimmy Wilde at the National Sporting Club, the rugged young Scottish champion told me all about his earlier days.

"I learned a' ma boxin', Maister Coarrie, in a boxin' booth, and never had what may be ca'd a lesson in my life. I just took on onybody that wud pit the gloves on to me. Sometimes I paid dearly for ma experience, gettin' mony a pastin'. It maittered naething to me what the weicht o' ma challengers was — licht - weicht, middle - weichts, or heavy-weichts—a' comers was the same taw me. Rough stuff, Maister Coarrie!

"Ye see, I hae aye been in the pink o' condeeshun: never smokit or drank in ma hale life. That's the thing that tells in the end. It keeps a mon's wind good and his nerves steedy. Boxers have tae be michty carefu' livers, if they want tae be any good at their bizness. I dinna ken what the taste o' bacca's like, or whusky either, although I'm a Scotsman. And there's mair Scotsmen like me than you Inglish think."

I told him I was an Irishman, and he apologized, adding, "That's a' richt, Maister Coarrie; there's mony a good Irishman—fine fechters, the Irish. Jim

Corbett is an Irishman, and so is John L. Sullivan. Ye see, I hae read a lot aboot the great boxers of the past. Boxin' mak's gran' readin'."

A goodly number of Lee's admirers travelled from Leith—I think it was—with their champion. And what a champion too!—beyond all doubt the best man Scotland has produced in my time. Lee's companions impressed me. They were a fine, intelligent, self-respecting lot of young fellows, a cut above the average fighting man's *entourage*. It amused and amazed them to find that Wilde was the favourite before the fight. They seemed to think the Londoners had more money than sense. I met them at Simpson's, in the Strand, where they all had lunch.

"I cannot understand what the betting means," said a smart young fellow, with his head screwed on the right way. "It's neither common sense nor logic. They must have forgotten who Tancy Lee is, and cannot have looked up his form. Fancy laying 5 to 2 on Wilde! I cannot see where it comes in, after the way Lee beat Percy Jones. Well, well! it's verra kind of them, and we're taking the odds they're laying and glad of it. We'll take their money, too, or I'm no Scotsman. We're risking a thousand pounds—a thousand pounds, war or no war."

"Ay, and takin' it back to Scotland three times ower, or near aboot it," said another. "We'll have the toon band oot to meet Tancy if he wins, and I hae nae doots aboot it. He'll be the first Scotsman tae tak' the Lonsdale Belt across the Border. We'll gi'e them ' Scots Wha Hae ' that nicht ! "

These were just the sort of fellows I like to see hanging around a boxer—sensible, nice youths, with no swank or swagger and no nonsense. To them the affair was a business proposition, interspersed with an unmistakable love of the sport. They were not going to be down-hearted if their man should be beaten—a possibility which could not for a moment be entertained on the merits of the case. I never saw a more splendid exhibition of confidence.

Lee himself was quieter than his supporters. "I'll win a' richt," was enough for him before the fight. Afterwards it was of Wilde he had most to say. " He was the gamest boy I ever met," said Lee. " My hands are sore with the punchin' I gave him. How he could take so much I dinna ken. It was like a fecht between a whippet and a Scotch terrier. I was the terrier, and had a' ma work cut oot to win. At times I was sorry for the plucky Welsh boy, but I never dare spare him ; he was so clever, and some of his punches were real stingers."

I don't suppose I ever saw the members of the National Sporting Club betray more real sorrow for a beaten man than they felt for Jimmy Wilde that night. The Welshman's seconds would have stopped the fight before it was half through, only that Wilde would have none of it. What must have been the courageous boy's feelings when compelled to surrender towards the end it would be hard to say.

But let it not be supposed from all this that Tancy Lee is a mere floundering fighter who hits out without judgment or science, and trusts for victory by a chance blow or that his opponent will ultimately be hammered to the boards. This would be no description of Lee's boxing, for boxing it is—on his own lines, if you like, but boxing none the less—all the way. He punches at all angles, and although he made free use against Wilde of the much-talked-of occipital punch, he always hit fair with the back of the knuckles. The occipital punch is well described by its other name, the "rabbit punch," derived from the way in which a gamekeeper puts a rabbit out of pain. It is struck on the back of the neck, at the base of the head.

I do not like the "rabbit punch," and it will not be my fault if one day—the sooner the better—it is forbidden. Nothing is easier than for this punch to be used in a foul way. Gunboat Smith is the great champion of it. He brought it into notoriety as Fitzsimmons made the solar-plexus blow famous. When Gunboat Smith lost his fight against Carpentier for hitting him when he was down, he employed the "rabbit punch." Nothing can be said for this back-of-the-head blow. It is always difficult, and often impossible, for the referee to see whether the blow is fairly or foully delivered; and, what is more, however often a boxer lands it, no points are given him for it. That fact should condemn it at sight.

I killed the kidney punch, unfortunately not before it had been attended with permanent injuries to more than one boxer. Freddy Welsh was the greatest of all kidney punchers. But the blow had to be disallowed for the honour of the sport, which was never intended to disable men for life. I shall kill the occipital punch, too, or I very much overrate my influence with those who regulate such things. Fatal results have already accrued from the blow, and as I argued in season and out of season for the abolition of the kidney punch, and in the end got my way, so I shall continue to denounce the "rabbit punch" till the hideous thing is banished from the art that is called noble.

No punch is legitimate unless it is delivered with the padded part of the gloves. I stopped a soldier from using the occipital punch quite recently, and I hope I shall not see much more of it, because I shall very likely stop it every time. I call it dangerous and contrary to the first principles of modern fisticuffs, which should see that boxing excludes, as far as possible, all risk of men permanently injuring each other's health. Temporary disablement is, of course, part of the game, but that a boxer should run constant risk of being crippled for the years that lie before him when his ring battles are over, does not commend itself to me. I leave those who defend the occipital punch to their own reflections. I have here stated my case for its prohibition.

I said that Tancy Lee used this punch in his fight

with Jimmy Wilde. The rules allow it and the boxer is justified, and I am sure that with or without it Lee would have beaten Wilde, who could not be expected, clever boy though he is, to give away the weight. Between heavy-weights, a stone of difference is neither here nor there; but between flyweights it is far too much, other things being about equal.

Fitzsimmons was middle-weight and heavy-weight champion at the same time, but there are seldom two men like Fitz in a generation.

It seemed a real pity to see such a lovely boxer as Jimmy Wilde get a hiding. And what a hiding! I forbear details. But he was not well when he met Lee, and should never have taken the ring. Wilde won a great triumph when he met Lee a second time.

CHAPTER VIII

SOME BOXING STORIES

ONLY once in my career have I witnessed a fight with the bare fists, a regular rough-and-tumble "knuckle-dust."

It took place in South London, between a Covent Garden porter and a Billingsgate porter, and was, I believe, the sequel to a public-house brawl. The stakes were five pounds aside. News of the fight reached the Stock Exchange, and a number of stockbrokers went down to see it. The names of the combatants I do not remember, and I am not sure that I should disclose their identity if I did.

It was a fight under old-time rules. In the case of the Covent Garden man, a powerful Irishman, science was conspicuous by its absence, and pluck very conspicuous by its presence. The Billingsgate porter was a Jew, with a pair of very clever fists, who fought on scientific lines, while his opponent trusted to strength and courage. The two men bore each other a grudge, and showed plenty of pugnacity. The fight lasted an hour and a quarter, and ran to anything up to a hundred rounds, though nobody kept count.

By "knuckle-dusting rules," fighting men could get to grips as they liked, combining wrestling with boxing. The Jew was an expert wrestler, and the way he threw his opponent about was comical to everybody but the Irishman. The floor of the room was boarded, and the rattle of the falling man's cranium sounded like a sledge-hammer driving piles. In due time both his eyes were closed, his nose was broken, his upper lip slit, the back of his head terribly bumpy; there was a swelling on his right jaw as big as an apple, and his body was black and blue. But his unconquerable spirit took no heed of his physical condition.

It was a combination of catch-as-catch-can and hit-as-hit-can, with a spice of scratch-as-scratch-can thrown in. I never saw any man mangle his opponent as that Jew mangled that Irishman. It might have been a case of a tiger settling a vendetta with a rhinoceros, the rhinoceros "taking the lot." The referee proved to be a most impartial judge of the contest, though the partisans, especially the Irishman's supporters, hurled uncomplimentary epithets at his head, and looked as if they might at any moment hurl more tangible missiles. Each time the Irishman was thrown his seconds, according to the old rules, picked him up, sat him on their knees, cooled and encouraged him, and then pushed him forward again into battle.

Presenting a most distressful spectacle, the Covent Garden porter towards the close of the fight lashed himself into a blind fury, and, rushing at his man, knocked him down with a thumping chance blow which happened to land in the pit of the stomach, completely doubling up the Israelite, who lay groaning and writhing in agony " on the boards."

His seconds implored him in vain to resume hostilities. He was not insensible to their entreaties. On the contrary, he was sensible enough to realize that the best thing he could do was to give up the fight before a worse thing happened to him.

"I don't want to be killed," he muttered, with the little wind left in his body.

His supporters turned from their defeated champion amid the jeers and cheers of the other side.

The conqueror stood over his victim in a contemptucus attitude, and this was what he said, speaking thickly and with great difficulty, owing to the dammed-up state of his mouth : "Gentlemen" —presumably addressing the stockbrokers,—" you have not seen me fight yet. This man's a quitter. I could have killed him. Get up, you coward, and let me knock you down again."

The " knuckle-dust " was followed by a tragedy, which resulted in the Covent Garden porter being sent to prison for life. That same night a man fell through an open window near Drury Lane, and the winner of the fight was arrested for pushing him through the window. He was convicted of murder, but the death sentence was commuted to penal servitude for life.

It always puzzled me that such an unmistakably

plucky fellow and game fighter should have been found guilty of the cowardly crime of pushing a man through a window several stories above the street. I suppose the Irishman was not in his sober senses when the deed was done.

An amusing incident happened while the fight was in progress. There came a rap at the door, and everybody whispered, amid a flutter of excitement, "Police!" Before the door was opened, two pairs of brand-new bright yellow gloves were fitted upon the hands of the fighters, with the object of proving to the representatives of the law that everything was all right and in order. We laughed at the ridiculous expedient, as the two men who had come through such a fierce encounter stood there wearing spotless gloves, which, of course, would have been in anything but a spotless condition had the fight been a legitimate glove contest.

The caller was not a policeman, after all, but only a belated stockbroker, who had followed us down to see the fight and missed it.

I never wished to see another "knuckle-dust."

Mr Alfred Bishop, the actor, is a cousin of mine, and his daughter, Miss Marie Lohr, becomes, I suppose, a half-cousin, or something like that. I received a telegram at my office one day inviting me to supper at the Savoy to meet Miss Lohr and Mr Loraine, the actor-airman. The wire was signed "Marie Lohr." Delighted with the invitation, I wired home for my best clothes and took a room at the Victoria Hotel, where, after a red-hot bath, I dressed myself up like a peacock.

On reaching the Savoy, I asked one of the waiters to direct me to Miss Marie Lohr's supper-party.

" I think you've made a mistake," said the waiter. " It must be the Carlton."

In hot haste, I made tracks for that hotel, preparing the most graceful apology for my being late. On the way out of the Savoy I ran against Mr Solly Joel, and begged him to excuse me, as I was in a great hurry to go and meet Miss Marie Lohr. Solly congratulated me on my good-fortune.

At the Carlton it was the same story. Miss Marie Lohr was not there, and there was no supper-party. I remembered that I had spoken to Mr Solly Joel some time before—proudly, no doubt—of my distant relationship to Miss Lohr, and then it all came to me in a flash that Solly had spoofed me! He always was a great practical joker.

Another practical joke, of which I have always suspected Solly's ingenuity, was of a rather gruesome description. It was well known that, despite my familiarity with boxing and its accompaniments, I have always had a horror of death. One day I was served with an official paper requesting my attendance as a juryman at a Coroner's inquest in Westminster. I trembled all over at the thought of having to visit the mortuary and inspect a dead body. Resolved to get out of the business if possible at all, I went round to Tom Honey, secretary of the Eccentric Club, and told him that I thought I should drop if I had to look at a corpse.

He said : " It will cost you a tenner to get out of it."

I said I should gladly pay twice as much if necessary. Tom thought ten pounds would do, and in due time I received another paper exempting me from the jury. I did not minutely examine these papers, but to my cursory glance they looked genuine. Tom Honey, Solly Joel, myself, and two or three friends celebrated the incident with a dinner at Romano's and a box at the Tivoli, the cost of the evening's enjoyment being defrayed by my ten pounds. Again I suspected Solly.

I was not done with Coroners' inquests yet. Once more a similar paper was served upon me, and my friends jocularly agreed that I could not expect to be exempted a second time at any price. That put the fear of death on me. On the day of the inquest I begged a friend of mine, Mr Freddy Clark, the director of the Hippodrome at Southend-on-Sea, to come with me to Westminster. We had a good many pick-me-ups on the way, as I felt in need of support to carry me through the ordeal. On reaching the Coroner's court, imagine my surprise and relief when the mortuary-keeper said : " We 'ain't got a corpse here of any description." To this day I believe Solly Joel was responsible for both these ghastly spoofs. He had " brought off the double."

SOME BOXING STORIES

My business relations with the Joel family began in a very simple way about twenty-five years ago, when I made the acquaintance of the late Mr Barnato, the South African millionaire, uncle to Mr J. B. Joel and Mr Solly Joel. Barney Barnato was a regular frequenter of the National Sporting Club. He said to me one Monday night: "Are you doing anything next Sunday?" I said, "No." He said: "Will you come to the house of my nephew, Mr J. B. Joel, at The Firs, Brondesbury? We are having a bit of sport."

The excellent programme included a professional boxing competition, and among the competitors were such well-known men as Jack Farley and Tom Ireland. Mr Barney Barnato came up to me after the spar and said: "What business are you in?" "I am with a firm of stockbrokers," I replied. "Hang me, if I don't give you some business!" I have dealt with the firm of Barnato Brothers ever since.

I remember that Barney never used to have more than a pound on a fight. He generally sat near the ring and made notes of the progress of the contest on his shirt-cuffs. He turned to me once while I was refereeing—outside the ring in those days—and said, looking at the marks he had pencilled on his cuffs: "How do you make 'em now?" This was at the National Sporting Club. "Oh no, I can't tell you that," I replied, laughingly. I think he liked me for that, because it was then that he invited me down to the house of Mr J. B. Joel.

J. B. had the reputation of being a very good fighter, and I remember that Barney invited me to put on the gloves to his stalwart nephew. It was a three-round bout, and it had not gone very far when I got the idea that J. B. meant knocking me out. We had just lunched previously, and sumptuously, so that I hardly felt in a condition for a serious bout. We both went at it very vigorously, and developed some respect for each other's fists. In the first round J. B. hit me a wallop with his right on the side of the head, the effect of which I could not conceal. I kept that blow in mind, and made it my business to keep out of its way for the rest of the time.

One of J. B.'s dangerous right-hand punches nearly came off in the last round, but I escaped from the bout, a loser on points, perhaps, but without having been knocked down. I imagine that J. B. would like to have been able to remind me to-day that he had knocked me out a generation ago.

Pugilists are fond of practical joking, and two clever examples come to my mind, the perpetrators being Willie Lewis and Tommy Burns, and their common victim Jewey Smith.

Willie Lewis was fighting Smith in Paris, and before the contest he went to the theatre as unconcernedly as if the fight was an affair of no importance. Lewis was only second to Carpentier in popularity with the Parisians. He always dressed well, and managed to

SOME BOXING STORIES

keep himself in fighting condition with a mimimum of training.

Shortly before his fight with Jewey Smith was timed to start, Lewis walked into Jewey Smith's dressing-room, wearing evening dress, patent shoes, an opera-hat, and white kid gloves, looking, in Smith's eyes, more of a popinjay than a pugilist.

There sat Smith bunched up in his chair, terrible to behold, with his broad back, his rolling shoulders and bovine neck that left scant room for a collar, his jaws set, and his mouth clenched, like a huge mastiff impatiently chafing for a fight. He had never seen Lewis before, and scarcely more than looked round when the toff, as he took him to be, said : " You're fighting a very good man to-night. You'll have to look out for yourself. Lewis is a pretty hefty fellah. I hope you're fit."

When Lewis had gone out, Smith said to his manager : " Who is that toff ? " The reply was : " That is the man you are going to fight."

Smith was staggered by the " gent's " coolness, and Lewis proved his words later by knocking the red-headed giant " all over the shop."

Cooler still was the conduct of Tommy Burns when he fought Jewey Smith in London. They were to meet in the office of Mr Will, the then editor of *Sporting Life*. Smith was jibbing at something or other in the conditions when Tommy Burns arrived wearing a top-hat and a gorgeous overcoat. Walking up to

Smith, he said: "Go on, sign these articles like a good fellow. Don't be a quitter. I will let you stay a round or two." I nearly exploded with laughter at the picture on Smith's face as he looked at the " knut " in front of him who had the nerve to speak these patronizing words. Tommy Burns, like Willie Lewis, proved in the ring that a man is no poorer a pugilist because he dresses like a gentleman. The Herculean strength of Jewey Smith was no match for the science of Tommy Burns.

If you were to look back to your youth, you would doubtless find some dominating personality that turned your boyhood in the direction of destiny. While yet in my teens I met the famous sculler and boxer, Billy Bone—" and muscle," as I used to say—of the North London Rowing Club, who became my hero as a boy.

" Do you box ? " he asked me one day.

" Not yet," I replied, " but I should very much like to try my hand at it."

" Done," said Billy. " Here is a pair of gloves for you."

I drew them on, and he put me through my first round, trouncing me quite soundly. From that hour boxing became my favourite pastime. I boxed with Billy Bone daily.

I am a Londoner out and out, with a tincture of Irish thrown in. Half a century ago I was born at Highgate, and thirty years of my life have been spent among the " Bulls " and " Bears " of Throgmorton Street. The firm of stockbrokers of which I am a partner to-day has been my firm from the first. I began as a stockbroker's clerk. But that was not actually my first venture into business. As a youth I used to walk daily from Hammersmith (to which place my people had moved) to Wellington Street, Strand, where I was employed in an architect's office. Regularly after my day's work I walked back to Hammersmith. I did not do this altogether to save money—though in all conscience money was scarce enough then—but by way of training and keeping fit.

To be strong and to have plenty of wind was my earliest ambition. I was always a worshipper of physical prowess, and my efforts to acquire it kept me out of mischief and indolent habits. The love of health and strength is the best guiding star a youth can have, in my humble opinion.

Not unnaturally, I may be prejudiced, but I do not apologize for my prejudices. I do not say a sound body is everything : I only say it is a pre-eminently good thing—one of the very best in the basket of life. It helps to the attainment of a sound mind—and to have both is ideal.

A nation of puny young men bodes ill for its old men. As my favourite English essayist, John Foster, somewhere says : " Why should a young man resolve to be cruel to the old man he expects to become ? " I am the father of four boys who have inherited my love of athletics. They are still little fellows, but it vastly amuses me to see them gloating over their muscular development, measuring their biceps, their chests, and the like.

There is no evening hour at home so pleasant for their mother and myself, or for visitors, I may add, as what we call the "Children's Hour." In the wide hall at the foot of the stairs my young hopefuls— "Toodles," Micky, Sidney, and John—don the gloves and pummel each other hard and cleverly. Even our four-year-old bantam, John, likes the sport quite as well as his elder brothers, and takes his knocks with splendid pluck. Rarely does any one of them manifest temper. That would be deemed very bad form, especially by Master John, who is a severe censor of his elder brothers' morals, and frequently tries his hand at refereeing. One day John may possibly follow in his father's footsteps. It was not necessary for me to force them to box. They are nurslings of the noble art. They took to it as naturally as the English schoolboy takes to cricket. I am not boasting that my young lions are better specimens of British boyhood than others, but they give me boundless satisfaction in physical respects anyhow, and I confess to being rather prejudiced in favour of the physical condition of the race. I hardly know whether I like better to see a "brainy" boy or a "brawny" boy.

Here is an appalling pun. Forgive me. A leader in the eugenic movement invited me some time

SOME BOXING STORIES

ago to favour him with my views regarding their doctrines. He addressed his envelope to me at Westcliff thus:

"EUGENIO CORRIE, ESQ."

I have never yet known a fighting man of any note who had not in him the elements of the " funny " man, and it would not be hard for me to turn these reminiscences into a collection of samples of boxing humour. Was there ever such a practical joker as Jem Corbett, variously styled " Gentleman Jim " and " Pompadour Jim," by reason of his fondness for fine clothes and of the manner in which he dressed his raven locks ?

Robert Fitzsimmons, the Cornish blacksmith, popularly known as Fitz, found fun in everything and everybody, though the expression on his freckled face, when pounding his mighty blows on Corbett's body during their classic contest at Carson City, might well have given any stranger the impression that his inborn ferocity banished every atom of humour from his composition. Though Fitzsimmons displayed none of the ordinary social amenities which belong to the wine-glass and the fragrant cigar, he was yet the most entertaining of associates, and rippled with fun and frolic all the while.

Even the stolid Jeffries, who stood heavily on his heels, erect, square-shouldered, firm of lip and jaw, had a quiet vein of chuckling humour, and invariably talked in the style of a man who thought it was great fun to be alive. A journalist friend of mine once interviewed Jeffries at the Waldorf Hotel, London, when all the white world were hoping and praying that he would prove the conqueror of Jack Johnson—which, as we all know, was a task beyond the gigantic American's prowess.

The interviewer and the pugilist were interrupted by a little baby who rolled up against Jeffries' legs like a ball of fluff. In a moment Jeffries picked up the child, and to the astonishment of the incoming and outgoing hotel guests, he dropped on his hands and knees on the carpet, and bade the journalist put the baby on his back.

They played at horses for half an hour, Jeffries remarking, " Babies always boss me." The newspaper man had to conclude his interview with a description of the incident, but it constituted the real tit-bit of his story.

The father of Jeffries was a preacher of the Gospel and travelled over a great part of the world as an evangelist. During the Boer War he visited London, and, being of a very swarthy appearance, he was surrounded by some youths in a West End street, who took him to be a Boer. Mr Jeffries, senior, sympathized with their antipathies and, after satisfying them of his American citizenship, promptly proceeded to preach to them, or " at " them, like a good evangelist who could not let such an opportunity go past him.

Jeffries used to tell this story with great gusto,

speaking of his father and himself as the preacher and the pugilist.

American humour is distinctive and very difficult to analyze or characterize. It is totally unlike Irish, Scottish or Cockney humour. I leave the task of defining it to any psychologist or literary anatomist who cares to take it on. One thing is certain, that the American pugilist, be he white or black, never hesitates to laugh at his own jokes. He may laugh first, laugh all the time, laugh last and laugh loudest. His laughter is infectious, and, so far from spoiling the joke, it brightens it.

Sam Langford showed himself to be both funny and far-seeing in conversation with me on one occasion. It was after a fight which I refereed in London between the stocky nigger and Bill Lang, the lanky Australian. We talked about the relative values of brains and brawn in a fighting man, and I happened to remark that Bill Lang had the reputation of fighting with his head, carefully thinking out his plan of attack as he went along.

Langford rolled his thick lips in a broad grin that revealed all the white teeth in his head, and said: "Mister Corri, he's pretty fast on his feet, but his brains ain't fast. While he was thinking I was hitting him."

Measured by its duration in seconds, the one-round bout between Wells and Carpentier at the National

Sporting Club, when the great White Hope of England fell to a rapid succession of blows in the region of his solar plexus from the marvellous French boy, was the shortest and most conclusive fight I have ever seen. It contrasted in a marked manner with a fight in America when one of the combatants, who had been requested by his father to cable the result immediately, sent the amusing and laconic message :

"Won easily. Seventy-five rounds."

Think of it ! Seventy-five rounds and yet "won easily " ! I hope they were not three-minute rounds. If they were, it would mean that the pugilists fought upwards of three and a half hours. How one of them came to win " easily " in these circumstances puzzles me. Perhaps the boxer who wired his sporting parent to this effect was an unconscious humorist. More likely he was still feeling a bit dazed when he sent the wire.

I, who tell so many stories about boxers and boxing, cannot complain if an occasional story is told about me and against me. That incorrigible wag, Jimmy Britt, the immaculately dressed and dapper little ex-light-weight champion of America, " got his own back," as the expressive saying goes, by relating the following to some of my friends, who retailed it to me with intense delight. This is how Britt tells the story. I give it in his own words, because any other style would spoil it :

SOME BOXING STORIES

"When I came over to England this last time I met Mr Corri in the Strand. He looked very hard at me. 'Now, Britt, you have made quite a lot of money boxing; haven't you, Britt?' I said, 'Yes.' Mr Corri said, 'Why don't you quit? You're beginning to show signs of what you are—a pugilist on the down grade, looking very old.'

"Anyhow, Mr Corri would insist on my lunching with him at the Savoy Hotel. We sat down at a table, and a little later two ladies and a man"—such was Britt's American expression—"came in and sat at the next table. They were continually looking over at our table.

"At last I heard one of the ladies say, 'Who is that at the next table?'

"I heard the man say, 'He's a pugilist.'

"The lady said, 'What a brutal face he has!'

"A little later on I heard the other lady say, 'Is he married?'

"The man said, 'Yes; that smart little fellow that is with him is his son.'"

Mine was the brutal face, if you please!

I suppose the ladies may be excused, not exactly for attributing brutality to my features, though they are possibly none too Grecian, but because the features of Jimmy Britt have none of the ferocity popularly ascribed to pugilists, and very erroneously in a great many cases. I pay Britt this compliment by way of returning good for evil. Jimmy pokes fun at you in the right way; you enjoy it as much as anybody else. It is a gift not to be acquired by prayer and fasting—least of all by fasting.

The following is a bright and shining "chestnut," and I imagine I have had a considerable hand in sending it on its rounds :

Jem Roche, the champion of Ireland, was fighting Frank Craig, the Coffee Cooler, in Dublin, an Irish referee in the ring. When time was called the Coffee Cooler promptly knocked Roche down with a beautiful right-hander. This is how the Irish referee started to count him out :

"One," said he. ("What the divil are you doing down there ? All you have to do is to give this nigger a punch in the stomach with your left hand and cross him with your right. You can do it.")

"Two." ("Think of your ancestors. They were lovely people. There's your old father sitting in front here ; do you want him to think you're a coward ? Get up, for the love of Ireland. You can't do 't.")

"Three." He went on in this way, and by the time he had counted five he had taken as many minutes.

Roche then got up and immediately set about the nigger like a mad bull and knocked him down. This is how the nigger was counted out :

"One, two, three, four, five, and five are ten. You are out, you great black baist !"

CHAPTER IX

MORE BOXING STORIES

IN the early days of my refereeing I used often to meet that famous pugilistic personage, Bob Habbijam, an old-timer and one of the most amusing men, I think, I've ever run against in the boxing world. I shall never forget Bob standing next to me when the late Curly Watson, who was unfortunately killed at Wonderland in a contest, gave an exhibition spar with some American boxer that had just arrived and was being given a trial to justify his claims upon the attention of London fight promoters.

The American had an enormous face, and Habbijam turned to me grinning with amusement, and said: "Law! look at Watson; they call him the coming champion of England. He's boxing with a man with acres of face, and he can't hit it."

It was Habbijam who on one occasion at his own boxing saloon, in Newman Street, Oxford Street, introduced two boxing men to the audience: "On the right, Massa Devonport, black. On the left, Bill Jones of Holloway."

"How many rounds, Bob?" called out one of the patrons of the place.

"It may be three, it may be a 'undred."

I was referee that night, and Habbijam came up to me and said, " Guv'nor, you'll have to give a decision; there's a lot of betting on it." The humour of the situation, of course, lies in the fact that it was an exhibition spar.

Habbijam had all kinds of boxers always coming to him for engagements ; those who had reputations to make, as well as those who had no reputations to lose. He told me that one day an " awful dirty-looking fellow " came to him and said he was the champion of Manchester.

" ' All right,' " said Habbijam, " ' I will give you a trial.' Without thinking what I was doing, I asked him into my lovely dressing-room. He took his socks off and threw them into a corner, where, on my word of honour, they stood up like Wellington boots ! "

When Frank Gardner and the Coffee Cooler fought at Wonderland, I went to Gardner's dressing-room and talked to him about the rules of the Ring, telling him what to do and what not to do ; not to hold with one hand and punch with the other, and so on.

" All right, Mr Corri," said Gardner. " I know all these things off by heart. I only want to ask you one favour. If this nigger fellow knocks me down, as long as I can get up again on my feet, and no matter how groggy I look, don't stop the fight. I have a wonderful way of recovering."

I have spoken of the one-round fight between Wells

and Carpentier at the National Sporting Club as possibly the shortest on record. I suppose it really was the shortest in the category of first-class bouts. But I have often met with cases in which an opponent has gone down at the first blow and remained down till he was counted out.

The fight between Tommy Burns and Jem Roche, the champion of Ireland, only lasted about fifteen seconds. It took place in Dublin, and a ready-witted Irishman turned a practical joke materially to his own advantage. Rushing out of the building, when the brief bout had ended, he affected great distress, and shouted to the crowd around the doors: " Does anybody want a ticket ? I cannot look at this fight any longer. Roche is killing him. You can have my ticket for £2, and chaip at the money."

He found a ready customer and quickly disappeared. The bidder's feelings may be imagined when he discovered how completely he had been done, the fight being over.

But for Irish wit and humour in the boxing world commend me to Father Herlihy, of South London. Two stories of the popular priest come to my recollection at the moment. A fellow with a very red nose stopped the good father in a street in Bermondsey, and pointing at his dog-collar, said : " Father, why do you wear a thing like that ? " The answer was pat and ready. " For the same reason that you wear that red nose—to show my occupation."

On another occasion a tipsy fellow made himself rather familiar with Father Herlihy, and for no apparent good reason said to him : " Father, can you tell me the quickest way to the infirmary ? " Thinking the man was " pulling his leg," the priest replied : " Just go down that street and turn sharp to the right into the court at the end of it, and shout as loudly as you can, ' To hell with the Pope ! ' and you'll be there in a minute."

The Stock Exchange once got up a boxing contest at the Kennington Social Club, and about forty cabs took the members down from the City Athenæum and the Thieves' Kitchen. Talking of the Thieves' Kitchen, by the way, a Frenchman who was taken there by a member looked alarmed when he heard the name of the place, and immediately started to take his pin out of his scarf. When he got in and saw the well-dressed and eminently prosperous-looking gentlemen present, he said : " Well, these are the most respectable lot of thieves I have ever seen."

I asked Spike Sullivan, training over here at the time to fight Jim Maloney—who afterwards became Bombardier Wells's manager—if he would spar for the entertainment of the stockbrokers. He said : " Yes ; git me a nigger."

The only nigger pugilist in London at the time was " Starlight," the celebrated Australian middleweight. Spike said, " He'll do," although he was giving about two stone away. They nearly murdered each other.

After the show we all went to supper at Gow's in the Strand, taking Spike Sullivan with us. During the meal Spike said : " Oh, I wish I was back at my training quarters. That nigger was hanging on to me all the time. I can smell him now."

Spike was training at the Two Brewers, Chipperfield, Herts. I said to him : " Are you game to walk there ? " It was a distance of about twenty-seven miles. He said : " Yes, if I can get anyone to walk with me." I said : " Come on, I will walk with you." I had on a frock-coat, a top-hat and patent-leather boots. I walked him all the way. We sent telegrams at different stages of the walk to Mr George Dunning, the great editor of the *Sportsman*, and he told the full story of the walk in his paper the next morning. The article was headed, " A Midnight Prowl. Mr Eugene Corri and Spike Sullivan walk to Chipperfield."

Most of us have done mad things in our time, and we are frequently heard rehearsing the doughty deeds of earlier days. Coming down from town to my home on the last train, with Tommy Sheard, the well-known Stock Exchange walker, to whom a " step " of anything from ten to twenty miles was a feat of no consequence, I asked him where he was going next day, and he said he proposed to walk to Clacton from Southend. I said I should like to accompany him, and, out of consideration for me, he altered his plans from Clacton to Billericay, the road being much better.

"When will you be ready ? "

"Now," I said.

There were several gentlemen in the carriage, and one of them, Mr Fred Clark, bet me the best dinner the Royal Hotel could provide that I would not finish the walk ; he to give the dinner if I did, and I to give it if I did not. All in the carriage were invited.

I had been at a dinner in town that night, and was more fit for my bed than a thirty-seven-mile tramp. We started from the Royal Hotel about one in the morning. I was wearing, as on the occasion of my " midnight prowl " to Chipperfield with Spike Sullivan, frock-coat, top-hat and patent-leather boots. Several sportsmen followed us in a " fly," drawn by a white horse, which covered every mile of the journey, there and back. We returned to the Royal Hotel about four o'clock in the afternoon, having well won the dinner. The patent boots played havoc with my feet, and I stopped a workman on the road and gave him a sovereign for the hobnail boots he was wearing. But these were much too big, so that I had to go back to my patents, enduring the agonies of the damned. I made the hotel-keeper a present of the workman's boots, and he put them in a glass case on which he stuck a label, telling how they came to be there. The white horse did not live long afterwards.

When Charlie McKeever the American fought Dido Plumb at the National Sporting Club, Mr John Douglas was referee, and I the timekeeper. Before the contest Mr Douglas said to me : " What an extraordinary man McKeever is ! I told him that if he knocked his opponent down, he must stand right back and let him get up. He looked at me and said : ' Well, in our country we do not usually kick him.' "

Strange and unaccountable things happen in the matter of pugilists turning the tables on each other. Jim Halloway and Jewy Cook fought at the National Sporting Club, two hundred pounds a side, and Mr J. B. Joel asked me to tell Cook that if he won he could have all the money. Mr Joel sent him to train at the Two Brewers, Chipperfield, Hertfordshire, bearing all expenses. Jewy Cook was beaten, and very shortly afterwards he fought Halloway again in South Africa and gave him a terrible scragging, much to Mr Joel's amazement.

A friend reminded me of an incident that had escaped my memory, and I tell it here for the humour that is in it. Coming out of the National Sporting Club one evening, I was stopped by an old pugilist of the " bruiser " breed. Looking very downcast and desperate, he said : " Guv'nor, I'm broke to the world. I've got the missus ill at home, and there ain't a crust in the cupboard. Could you let me have a shilling or two, and God bless you ? " I gave him half a dollar, and he beamed with gratitude, saying: "Thank you, guv'nor; bli' me, what a funeral you'll have! Pity you won't be alive to see it."

Droll fellows these old pugilists are, and good-hearted in the majority of cases. Standing at Romano's bar one day, Jim Carney insisted on buying me a drink. "All right, Jim, I'll have a French and Italian vermouth and gin," I said. "Right, guv'nor," said Jim, walking up to the bar, and throwing out his chest. Looking puzzled, he came back, and said: "Do you mind ordering it yourself?"

A Billingsgate man had been counted out, and was pulling himself together with difficulty, when one of his supporters leaned over him and asked sympathetically: "'Ow did it feel to 'ear the referee counting you out?" The defeated man replied: "Just like tallying aht boxes of kippers at the market."

"Is there anybody else wounded?" asked another prostrated pugilist, coming to his senses after having been put to sleep. "I thought the house had fallen in."

The following must surely be a unique "knock-out." It is told of a waiter at the Falcon Hotel, Southend, who was reading the account of the great fight between Jack Johnson and Tommy Burns at Sydney. So engrossed was he in the vivid description, that he forgot his surroundings and commenced

MORE BOXING STORIES 155

making gestures as the account of the fight progressed. The writer dwelt at length upon the manner in which Johnson played for the "knock-out," and when the waiter reached the description of the final punch, he imitated it so precisely that he actually jabbed the point of his chin with his right fist and knocked himself off his chair!

An amusing example of bluff among boxers, practised especially by American boxers, is told of Willie Lewis when he fought in Paris. Going into Pat O'Keeffe's dressing-room immediately before the contest, he started chaffing him about his appearance, and, pointing at the big fellow's stomach, he said : "You're a ver' good fella, but you can't go into the ring with a stomach like that ; if I hit you there I might kill you, and I don't feel like going on with the contest until you've trained that down a bit." His opponent protested that he was all right, and that he was not bulging with fat, but with muscles. Lewis, however, persisted until the fellow got his stomach on the brain, so that when they squared up in the ring he immediately guarded it with his left forearm, leaving himself exposed to Lewis, who promptly hit him a terrific punch on the point. "Outed" by bluff!

I have noticed many curious things about boxing men—notably that they are almost all superstitious and carry mascots about with them in the shape of pets, baubles, and trinkets, given to them by particular friends, or wives or sweethearts.

As everyone knows, women are not admitted to the National Sporting Club. Manly art though boxing is, the spectacle of men fighting is not for feminine eyes.

Once a woman came to the Club precincts from a remote London suburb; she had walked all the way. Her husband was inside—in the ring, as a matter of fact—but he did not know his wife was outside in the street. Perhaps he never got to know; more than likely she never told him. This woman's husband was a notable pugilist, though his name must be suppressed here. He was fighting that night for love and money; he was in straitened circumstances, and had a child ill at home. I doubt if his wife had a shilling in her pocket as she remained outside, gliding among the shadows from one part of the building to another, listening to the cheers and counter-cheers, trying to gather how the tide of battle—the tide of fortune in her affairs—ebbed and flowed.

Imagine the agonizing suspense of that wife and mother. She had left her ailing baby in charge of a sympathetic neighbour and followed her husband to town, so insupportable was her anxiety on her bread-winner's account. Well, her husband was beaten—not badly, but beaten is beaten, and a moral victory brings small consolation to a defeated man, or his wife and family in dire need.

The fight at the Ring between Fred Storbeck, the Boer blacksmith, and Frank Moran of Pittsburg, the great fighting dentist, is still fresh in my memory. If ever a boxer had his second to thank for winning a fight, Moran had on this occasion. The dentist was seconded by Dan McKettrick, who afterwards became Young Ahearn's manager. It was a twenty-round contest, and ended in the nineteenth round, when Storbeck was stopped, to the amazement of everybody. Two rounds before the surprising finish Storbeck had won easily on points, and Moran looked as if he couldn't have knocked over a tailor's dummy.

The dentist, I believe, was going to stop, when his shrewd second called out to him : " Walk round, Frank, walk round. He's awful tired like to drop."

Storbeck tired ! The Boer was going as strong as a springbok. But Moran was too far gone to see this, so he believed McKettrick and took heart again.

The ruse of the ingenious second succeeded. Moran walked round and round the ring, keeping out of Storbeck's way and gathering his wind. After the minute's interval he came up for the eighteenth round a new man. In the nineteenth round Storbeck's seconds " threw the towel " in literally.

I said to McKettrick : " That fight was won by you and nobody else." He looked at me as much as to say : " I know it was, and who had a better right ? "

There have been few greater managers or seconds than this same McKettrick, who studied the men in his care till he knew what they could do better than they knew themselves. The boxer who has found a good manager, like the man who has found a good wife, is decidedly in luck's way. Carpentier, for example, would have been a great boxer under anybody's management, but nothing like such a great boxer as he became under the devoted and affectionate care of Descamps.

McKettrick seconded Young Ahearn when he fought Braddock, who, like a good patriot, rejoined his regiment directly war was declared. He also seconded Jeannette, against whom Colin Bell, the Australian Bushman, put up such a good show at Premierland, in the presence of Billy Wells, who a few weeks later knocked Bell out, and so brought to an inglorious end the uneventful visit of Bell to England, where he made a lot of friends, but added little to his reputation as a boxer.

Cool as a cucumber, and an excellent judge of boxing and boxing men, McKettrick always maintained that Young Ahearn would have beaten Gunboat Smith. " Smith was made for him," he would say. " The Gunboat was too slow ever to hit a clever boy like Ahearn." He was not so confident when Wells or Carpentier was mentioned.

How often, how very often, have I refereed fights when it was a " million to one " against the man who yet won from sheer perseverance and pluck ! The saying applies more to boxing than to any other sport, that a match is never won till it is finished.

In proof, there is the great fight between Ted White and Billy Murphy of Australia at the National Sporting Club some years ago. For nineteen rounds Murphy was " Receiver-general." He took the lot with hardly a point to his credit, all the way. White virtually knocked himself out punching his opponent. In the end Murphy slung a right hand and hit White with such terrific force on the back of the head that he fell on his face and could not get up.

The blow did not render him unconscious. It was simply a case of a prostrated man who had so exhausted himself punishing an opponent that he had not enough strength left to get upon his feet. All through the fight it seemed as if White couldn't miss Murphy, who justified his reputation as a cast-iron man.

" He is unnatural, Mr Corri," said White to me afterwards. " I needed a battering-ram to knock him out. A shillaly wouldn't have done it."

Bombardier Wells has contributed pretty freely to the surprise packets of the ring. The two soldiers, Sunshine and Voyles, were both knocked out by Wells after they had brought him to a state bordering upon collapse, and his supporters to the verge of despair.

Some boxers are endowed with wonderful powers of recovery. The way in which they suddenly pull themselves together from the most pitiable conditions is an eye-opener to the spectators and an object-lesson to their opponents.

The unexpected happens both ways. The boxer who is making rings round his opponent, doing as he likes with him, sending his supporters into ecstasies of delight, often unexpectedly measures his length on the floor, in blissful ignorance of the tumult that rages round him.

Smith, Palzer, and Carpentier (the last-named in his first fight with Wells at Ghent) were all outboxed and outclassed by the Bombardier in the first rounds, and men were laying heavy odds on him. But they lost their money, and non-partisan lovers of boxing had the mortification of seeing the best man beaten by the knock-out blow within the space of a few minutes.

So it was when Moir put Wells out at Olympia. In the first round the Gunner was down about half a dozen times. People were preparing to leave the place, not caring to witness such a one-sided affair. In the second round Moir landed a punch which upset all calculations.

Of course, it is true that a mere boxing match may be a rather insipid spectacle. Most men like to see real fighting, and would not waste any sympathy upon the scientific boxer who played for points all the time and finally got knocked out by a man who had taken the punishment meted out to him and yet remained capable of writing " paid " to all the points against him. The boxer who is no fighter stands very little higher than the fighter who is no boxer.

In this connection I shall always remember my

MORE BOXING STORIES

first and only experience of the pitmen of Tyneside, of whose sporting tendencies it was said, when the local authorities proposed some drastic measures to stop gambling, that they would bet on " two straws on the river."

The best heavy-weight at the time was Ben Taylor, known as the Woolwich Infant. A ponderous, big fellow of the John L. Sullivan class, his admirers gave him this nickname by way of a joke. In the North they had a good man, George Crisp of Newcastle, and between these two a fight was arranged for the heavy-weight championship of England.

There were no Lonsdale Belts in those days, and it was not necessary, as it is to-day, for belt championships to take place at the National Sporting Club. Taylor and Crisp fought in the Standard Theatre, Gateshead, and the place was full of pitmen. It was a novel spectacle to me.

I can see those pitmen now, at fever-heat of excitement all the time, sitting for most part in their shirt-sleeves, and partaking freely of refreshments where they sat. I can hear them, too, jeering and shouting, as their feelings were stirred one way or the other. It was a never-to-be-forgotten fight.

The miners liked it all the better for its fury. Men who earned their money—and good money, too— by hewing coal from the hard facings of the mine, might be pardoned for preferring a fiercely contested bout to a boxing display. I hope, however, they were not all quite so ferocious as the fellow with the stentorian voice who shouted the moment time was called : " Go on, Geordie ! Kill him ! Kill the referee ! Kill anybody ! "

Never having refereed on Tyneside before, I had a certain feeling of loneliness in the midst of that crowd of rugged pitmen ; but they followed the fighting so closely and knew so much about good work when they saw it, that it became a pleasure to referee before them. I had no friends in Newcastle when I arrived, but made many during that short visit, coming away with a tremendously high opinion of Novocastrian hospitality. Best of all, I remember my host, Jimmy Lowes.

Fortunately, Crisp neither " killed " his opponent nor " killed " the referee. He won the fight about the eighth round, to the mad delight of the pitmen, who, if they would bet on " two straws on the river," would be still more likely to bet on " two men in the ring."

It was a great night on Tyneside, for a " Geordie " had won the heavy-weight championship of England —an event about equal to the " United " winning the Cup at the Crystal Palace. I met so many "good sports " in Newcastle that I have often wished to renew my acquaintance with the place. What a fine race these Durham and Northumberland men are ! In the saloon bar of a leading hotel I drew a friend's attention to about a dozen men standing around, whose height ranged from six feet to six feet three or four—fresh-complexioned giants every one.

MORE BOXING STORIES

Another Tyneside man, Jack Curley of Newcastle, made a grand show in a fight at the National Sporting Club with Jack Roberts, the Drury Lane bulldog, for the feather-weight championship. It looked any odds on Curley all the way till Roberts knocked him out a minute after a bet of £100 to £1 was made on Curley.

Oh, these " million-to-one " certainties ! They almost seem to go wrong as often as they come off.

Two novices made a sensational start at the Club. Both led off vigorously with their right hands, landing resounding blows. One happened to catch the other on the point of the jaw and knocked him down. He was counted out before the bout had gone a minute. His seconds went into the ring and carried him to his corner, all of a heap.

They pulled his ears, slapped his cheeks, and poured cold water down his back in their efforts to bring him round, doing everything that would have made him dangerously cross had he been in his senses. It was several minutes before they succeeded, and in the meantime his opponent had left the ring, postponing the formality of shaking hands. When the beaten man revived, he looked across the ring, and, seeing nobody there, he turned to his seconds and asked : " Where is he ? 'As he give in ? "

Fighting men all tell that from the moment of the " knock-out " blow till the moment of waking everything is a blank. There is no sleeping-draught like a punch on the point, and no sleep so sound and dreamless.

In his own way the referee is oblivious to all that goes on in the audience. Only the most unusual incident attracts his attention. With him it is " eyes front " and " mark your man " all the time.

Once at a London boxing resort, a fool of a fellow in the audience drew a revolver and threatened to shoot me. They took the revolver from him after a scuffle, so they told me afterwards, for it was not till then that I knew anything of it. I suppose if the madman had fired I might have heard the shot, perhaps even felt it. The manager keeps the revolver as a " souvenir."

I have met some funny fellows in my time and had some rum experiences, but I never like to think of that night which might have put me to sleep. Only a few days ago I met a sporting journalist, who promised to let me see a proof of my obituary notice, which he had written and got ready in cold type, when I was believed to be wavering between two worlds with pneumonia. One's own obituary should make rather eerie reading !

Another creepy sort of story crops up here. Two men called at my office to ask whether I could help a certain old-time boxer, who was very far down in his luck. Times were good on the Stock Exchange then, so that it must be years ago. I collected thirty pounds on 'Change in thirty minutes. Next day the same two old " sports " called again, this time to say very dolefully : " Oh, Mr Corri, where would you like our old friend to be buried ? "

I replied : " I am so sorry. Poor old chap ! Is he dead ? "

Imagine my surprise when they said quite seriously : " No, not yet ; but you have been so kind, we thought you'd like to choose the cemetery ! "

That was all they said, and I have been puzzling ever since to know what they meant. Apparently they could think of nothing more to say at the time, and that was the last I saw or heard of them. I do not know now whether the old-timer is alive or dead.

What a time I had in the early months of the war ! Refereeing might have become my profession, instead of a recreation that makes life worth living, so many and urgent were the calls upon my services at boxing exhibitions and contests in all parts of England and Wales.

Wherever soldiers, Territorials, and Kitchener men were training for the great final struggle on the Continent, boxing was their favourite pastime.

" If you have any papers to send the men who are getting ready to die for you," said an officer to me, " let them be papers that contain stories of great glove fights. These will be devoured. It is no time for sentimental novels or other food for babes. The fighting mood wants fighting food."

Accompanied by Mr Bettinson of the National Sporting Club, Mr George Dunning of the *Sportsman*, Mr James Hulls of *Sporting Life*, and Mr Rushton of the *Daily Express*, I went down to Shoeburyness one afternoon to see Johnny Summers going through his gymnasium work for his championship fight at the National Sporting Club with Johnny Basham. He had for sparring partners Jem Roche, Curley Walker, and an ample supply of soldiers from the barracks.

I witnessed one of the most remarkable knock-outs ever seen. Summers, who always trains vigorously, hit Roche on the jaw, causing him to fall sideways on his head and then roll over, for all the world like a shot rabbit, except that he made his strange somersault.

CHAPTER X

BOXING IN THE WAR

OF all sports during the War none lived a more lusty life than boxing, none thrived so, none ate itself more surely into the affections of the people ; and now we may say with complete certainty that it has come into its kingdom.

It is true that it has yet to be legalized, but it is not any hole-and-corner business. We may and do practise it with the approval and sympathy of everybody. The very people who before the war professed to see in glove fighting only viciousness, now applaud it, for the war has killed that species of littleness which only begets misunderstanding.

Until almost the eve of the war it was said that unless the youth of Britain was weaned of his fondness for sport he would fall in the race of the nations for supremacy ; that sport had become an obsession ; that it was scotching the wheel of progress. And there were times when, if I had not known it to be otherwise, I should have said that we were on the brink of degeneracy ; that we were perilously near becoming an effete nation.

But you know what has happened.

Did not the passion for sport have most to do with making the most glorious army the world has ever known ? Has not sport the greatest Roll of Honour ? Has not sport—this wonderful thing conceived for the making of men—been the greatest factor in winning the War ? Had not our boys played games from their toddling days, and so acquired that initiative, self-reliance, and adaptability which games teach, from whence would have come the greatest fighting force in all history ?

At different times during the War I was invited to offer my opinion on the value and the necessity of sport, and more particularly boxing. At a period when we were enthralled by the magnificent gallantry of our boys, when they were holding up against the German hordes, when it was feared that sheer weight of numbers would crush them, and when, too, the world was shocked and sickened by the barbarities of our enemies, I ventured to declare that our boys would pull through because they were sportsmen—that their inborn love for games would sooner or later send the Germans back reeling and broken.

Germany was crumpled because she never knew the meaning of sport, and never practised it. She was a bully because she held aloof from hard games.

Do you know that Germany has never reared a boxer with any pretensions to class ? For years I was a member of the German Gym., but, although boxing there was counted a great sport, not one single German within my memory ever stood up in the ring to fight. The Germans excelled in physical drill, in fencing and the like ; but, because boxing finds out a man more readily and surely than any other sport, they would have none of it. In the mass the Germans cut an imposing figure ; individually they were cowards and bullies.

From the first day that a training camp was set up in this country right down to the days of the Armistice, I had the privilege of refereeing at nearly every military centre. Wherever soldiers were there was boxing. Officers and men alike insisted on boxing. At home, and behind the lines, and on the high seas there was boxing continually even during the darkest days of the war ; officers and men took the ring. And the war, instead of killing the passion for games, intensified it.

When war broke out we decided to tuck away our sports as we understood and played them in peace time. It was right and proper that we should do so. But the National Sporting Club, as personified by my old friend, Peggy Bettinson, said that there would be days and nights when sport must have its fling ; that our armies, being built up of sportsmen, would fly to sport at every conceivable opportunity ; and how abundantly the policy of the National Sporting Club in carrying on throughout the war was justified we all know.

It is true that we were denied a succession of international contests, but we had fighting that was better than it had ever been done before. It was more interesting. It had more humanity in it. It was more natural. The National Sporting Club did a noble work.

Now the general public do not regard it as merely the home of fisticuffs; it now ranks among our most worthy institutions. It said : " Sailors and soldiers of all the countries welded together to win this war for right and justice, you may come here and be entertained." And they came in battalions. There took the ring at different times many " unknowns," to demonstrate and to prove that our boys did their boxing better than ever we suspected they could do.

Better still, for nearly five years many noble charities were enriched. Thousands of pounds were raised by boxers and boxing men. There was the British Sportsman's Ambulance Fund, by which a fleet of cars were distributed among the different theatres of war.

It is not, however, possible to enumerate the patriotic and charitable works of the National Sporting Club. The Club was a fountain of practical goodness, and I do hope that at some time or other we shall be given a record of its war work. That its Roll of Honour is a long and glorious one goes without saying. The N.S.C. bred many great and noble soldiers, and boxers generally played their part like real men.

I have not been able to keep a record of notable boxers who made the great sacrifice. They are so many. But out of the glorious list of heroes there now pass before my mind two men who grip my imagination tighter than perhaps any of the long line of the fine young fellows.

I knew so well Norman de Crespigny (about whom I have told in this book) and the Reverend Hulton-Sams.

To know any of the de Crespignys is to know the best type of sportsman. Sir Claude stands at the head of an uncommon race. He has been a fighter all his life. The spirit of daring, the love of adventure and chivalry are deep down in him. Norman was a worthy son of a worthy sire. I know how he would go down. He would go down fighting to the last gasp. As he was in the ring, so he must have been in the war, a gallant.

I would not have you believe Norman de Crespigny was a greater hero than any of the other sportsmen who have gone from us. I would have you only believe and accept him as typical of the Britisher, of the boxer, of the sportsman.

And so, too, was poor Hulton-Sams. Like de Crespigny, I had come to regard him as one of my boys, for in many of his fights at school and the 'Varsity I acted as referee. Hulton-Sams could not help fighting if he had tried. He looked what he was— a fighter, and the last example of a muscular Christian.

In the ring he used to fight until he dropped. When his 'Varsity days were over he took up a curacy in the Midlands. Later he went to Queensland, and when war broke out his "flock" were hard, unconventional men. He preached the Gospel to them by being one of them. He would fight with the best of them. Any of them could have a scrap with him. He was literally the "fighting parson." Men of the Bush just loved him. And when war broke out he bid them farewell. He was refused a chaplaincy. So he came over—I believe in a cargo-boat,—enlisted as a private, won commissioned rank, and died leading his boys into action. His death was the death he would have had—the death of a fighter.

But, as I have said, there were many Norman de Crespignys and Hulton-Sams among the boxers in the War. Were I to tell you about them all, I should require a whole book in which to spread out my story.

In the terribly long Roll of Honour you may find the names of boxers from all the corners of the earth. Good John Hopley came pell-mell from Rhodesia when his young brother—also the champion heavy-weight at his school and 'Varsity—had been killed. And no sooner had he reached the front than he won the D.S.O.

But I would not enlarge further upon the boxing heroes. They are countless.

I would tell, so far as possible in the limited space at my disposal, of the features of the game as I saw them.

First, as I have mentioned, every sailor and soldier becomes a boxer, and now boxing in the services is done in a way that would have rejoiced the heart of my dear old friend, Sir Malcolm Fox, the father of Navy and Army boxing, whose death we all so deeply regretted.

The Services Tournament, spread over two days at the Albert Hall, was, to my thinking, the greatest event that has ever occurred in the history of boxing. The King, ever ready to encourage all men-making games, gave a trophy which, but for indisposition, he would have presented to the winning team in person. Prince Albert, in the presence of fully ten thousand people, with nearly all the world's most notable fighters drawn up in the ring, deputised for His Majesty, and from that moment we felt that boxing had been brought into line with all the sports.

We shall never see the like of the Albert Hall Tournament again, for the reason that it will not be possible to bring together into the same ring so many famous boxers, who fought for glory and honour, and with an enthusiasm and determination the professional pugilist would only be expected to show were he fighting for a bulging purse. There was only a medallion to be won, and yet for two whole days, with the world looking on, they fought with all the hardness that was in them.

It was a tournament in which the soldier-boxers of all the Allied countries appeared. The King's Trophy was won by the British Army, with the American forces runners up. I do not propose to tell of all the bouts. Merely will I recall what appealed to me as the most impelling features.

Perhaps first I should treat with the defeat of Jimmy Wilde by the American sailor, Pal Moore. Wilde had previously disposed of Joe Lynch—whom he afterwards met at the National Sporting Club—and Digger Evans, a hard-hitting, rugged little fellow from Australia.

To my amazement, Wilde, who in my judgment won each of the three rounds, was declared to have lost. Most people were dumbfounded, and there was loud and long disapproval. I cannot explain how it came about that the judges decided that Moore won. It was two against one. That they arrived at such a conclusion with every honesty no one would deny. What happened was that they blundered, and I should very much like to see Wilde and Moore with smaller gloves than those used in the tournament over the championship course. To my thinking, Moore is not such a good boxer as Lynch, who, it may be mentioned, afterwards outpointed our fly-weight champion, Tommy Noble, in a contest at the Ring, Blackfriars.

The form of all the countries at Albert Hall was excellent—that of Great Britain and America the best. The two countries had a rare race for the King's Trophy. Billy Wells, whose subsequent defeat by Joe Beckett I shall refer to later, proved to be the best of the heavy-weights, and after seeing him against Eddie McGoorty, I was almost prepared to believe that at last he had learned to conquer his temperamental weaknesses. Eddie McGoorty is not

BOXING IN THE WAR

a heavy-weight strictly speaking, but he is still a great boxer and fighter.

Of all the Americans I liked Mike O'Dowd the best. A middle-weight really, he dared to measure his strength against the light heavies, and he was the winner. This O'Dowd, judged by appearances, is the fighting man *in excelsis*. Face much battered, hair cropped close, one of his ears telling eloquently of a life of fighting, he had something about him that took us all to him. He fought fiercely, and yet there was never any suggestion of vice in him.

Quite a character Mike O'Dowd is, and I saw that afterwards, when in Paris, after a fighting tour in Italy, he challenged Georges Carpentier. He believes that he can beat the Frenchman, but I can scarcely agree with him. If they did meet, however, I am sure the tussle would be a rare one; O'Dowd must be kind of killed before he would think of quitting.

Some little time before the Albert Hall Tournament an affair which excited quite a lot of interest, but one which did not win generous patronage from the public, was a fight at the Chelsea Football Ground between Jimmy Wilde and Joe Conn, a young Hebrew who, up to that time, had come to be regarded as about the best feather-weight we had.

It was said, and with some show of reason, that Wilde, wonder though he unquestionably is—I maintain that he is the most remarkable boxer of this or any other age,—was taking on the greatest proposition of his life in consenting to meet Conn. For this Conn up to this period had shown that he was quite an extraordinary boxer, clever, clear-thinking, and so far had done all that was expected of him. He is taller than Wilde, and, of course, much heavier. Behind Conn were about the shrewdest people in the world of boxing, and they believed that their man would lower the colours of the Welshman.

This is what happened :

Conn, who had been spoken of as a youngster of much cunning and with heaps of talent, was so outclassed that we could scarce believe our own eyes. Not only so ; he seemed scared, and at no time did he do more than cover up. Wilde, by his showing in this contest, proved that he was not only a wonder, but positively uncanny.

I have seen all the little men during more years than I care to remember, and I declare that there has never been any like him. He is a freak, just as Bob Fitzsimmons was a freak, as Griffo was a freak, as most of our marvellous fighters were freaks.

When he had beaten Conn, Wilde gave it out that his next fight would be in America, but he changed his mind. Immediately the Armistice was signed, it was obvious that London was to be the boxers' El Dorado, just as it was in 1914.

I am writing when London is full of fighters, and when the odds are that we shall have them coming from all parts of the world for some time to come. My old friend Charles Cochran has come into the game. He it was who gave to us the first big fight since the War—I mean a fight that got hold of the public imagination.

As the proprietor of the Holborn Stadium—a hall in the very centre of London where in the days of my youth many famous men of the Ring appeared—he got hold of Billy Wells and matched him against Joe Beckett, of Southampton. And he made this arrangement also—the winner was to meet a Guardsman named Frank Goddard, a mountain of a man, some twenty-three years of age, and one Sir Claude de Crespigny thinks no end of; and the reappearance of the Bombardier, especially after his defeat of such a seasoned fighter as Eddie McGoorty, took London by storm.

The shrewd Cochran gave it out that his purpose was to find the best of the British heavy-weights, and in the autumn match him against Carpentier, rightly regarded as the European champion, at Olympia. As a matter of fact, before he had signed Wells and Beckett up he had sent out one of his agents and got Carpentier to enter into a contract whereby he would have his first fight since the war under his auspices and against the man who had been proved to be the best.

By the way, when war broke out, Carpentier was a millionaire in francs, but the greater part of this sum was invested in the coal-mines round about his home at Lens, so that when he comes back to the Ring he will be as a man after making another fortune.

His manager, Descamps, is very rich. Rejected for

the French army, he took over a modest little factory at Le Guersche, and as a manufacturer of boxes in which to pack Camembert cheeses he has made quite a pile of money, and I should say that he is about one of the wealthiest men who has ever managed a boxer.

When Cochran had made a match between Wells and Beckett, he secured permission for Carpentier to visit England, and the Frenchman, now twenty-five years of age, appeared at the ringside dressed in khaki, with his tunic generously decorated with medals he had won on the field of battle.

Carpentier, who sat by the side of the Duc d'Orleans, was invited into the ring, and he was given a tremendous reception. He said to me afterwards : " It is very hard to believe that I am a Frenchman, for whenever I come amongst you, you frighten me with your welcome. You are given to saying that you English are very cold and formal, but it cannot be. You can be just as demonstrative as the Frenchman."

Wells was beaten by Beckett in the fifth round. And again it was all a " tragedy of the Bombardier." Now, Wells had already beaten Beckett, and though I, like a good many more, have always been prepared for Wells buckling up, I did think that he would win this time. But the moment he came into the ring I saw that he was in for a beating. Not that there was anything wrong with his condition, but it was as clear as daylight that he had, as always, developed an attack of nerves.

Wells has set it down in print that he lost because he was pursued by Fate. Nothing of the kind. He was beaten by a man on the night's showing who was a better fighter. There was none of "the waist of a woman and a jaw of glass about him," as was once said by an American writer. He just did not have it in him to beat the other fellow. As near as possible he was beaten by the very first punch, for he was at once sent sprawling, and the surprise was that he got up and lasted until the fifth round.

I am now certain that Wells is not made of the stuff that goes to make a champion. He is not a coward by any manner of means. He simply is not cut out for the fighting game. There are those who are saying and writing, the while I am offering this opinion of Wells, that he is sure to come back. Indeed, the likelihood is the public will insist that he should be given another try to make good. Never in the whole course of my career have I known a parallel to Wells. No boxer with any pretensions to class has had a more sympathetic public or a larger one, and within a few hours of his defeat by Beckett folk were saying: "Poor Billy! Never mind; he will yet show that he is the best of the bunch."

But I must not write any more of Wells, though the temptation to do so is hard to resist. How many columns of matter have been written about the Bombardier?

Shortly before the Wells and Beckett affair we learned that the Committee of the National Sporting

Club, recognizing the immensity of public interest in boxing and the fact that the fighting at Covent Garden must of necessity be done before a limited audience, had decided to take over the old skating-rink at Holland Park and use it for the big international contests, and to provide accommodation for twenty to thirty thousand people. This building is to be an annexe of the old Club, and now, in the future, the N.S.C. can give to the world at large an opportunity to see boxing under the best possible conditions.

In other words, it will not be left entirely to the enterprise of any individual to introduce to the general public world championships. It is a bold policy that the old Club has embarked upon, but I feel sure that it is one that will do much to keep boxing one of the most popular of all sports. With Holland Park fitted up in the way intended, the N.S.C. will be able to compete with the most daring promoter in the world.

There is now no reason that the next fight for the heavy-weight championship should not be at Holland Park. I do not expect that the N.S.C. will follow Tex Rickard and offer goodness knows how many thousands to the champion, but it will be able to give to the best and most famous boxers exceptionally generous terms. I am glad the N.S.C. is to launch out, and I can only believe that its enterprise will meet with a handsome reward. There should be a succession of championships under the ægis of the home of British boxing. But what is wanted more than anything else is for the Board of Control to realize its purpose and to give to boxing the equivalent of the Jockey Club—or, if you like, set up an M.C.C. of boxing. In other words, a properly constituted government that will be recognised by the world.

Lord Lonsdale hopes—and there is no reason to suppose that his hopes will not be realised—to bring about by means of his belts something that would be very much like a regular series of inter-country fights. As far as I have been able to ascertain at the moment of writing, his lordship will offer to the world's boxers a belt for each of recognised weights. These weights to be fixed and agreed upon by the Board of Control. This is the idea :

At the National Sporting Club or at the Holland Park Skating Rink a belt will be put up for competition, say, between England and America. If it were won by a Britisher, then twelve months later it would be competed for in the United States, perhaps at Madison Square Gardens. If this idea were realised, then every year home-and-home " internationals," as in cricket, as in football.

The project as yet has not taken definite shape, but when it is put before the sporting public it is sure to be heartily supported. *Apropos* the giving of £5000 to Carpentier, and following the statement that the giant cowboy, Jess Willard, had been promised £20,000 to defend the title he won at Havana from Jack Johnson, to get into the ring with Jack Dempsey, we shall be regaled with articles decrying huge purses and bewailing professionalism in sport generally.

That boxing must have professionals is obvious, for it must be the professional who will teach and set a standard of skill.

I am opposed to commercialism in any sport if that commercialism tends to sordidness; but so long as boxing—be it for big or little money—is well and decorously done, I don't care one way or another whether men fight for big or little purses.

Supposing it were decided that no man should fight for more than a few hundred pounds. If it chanced that a boxer was one that all the public desired to see, the promoter would get all the halfpence and the boxer all the kicks.

Whatever be said to the contrary, the popular scrapper occupies very much the same position as any public performer.

He draws the people to him and, by reason either of his personality or skill, they willingly put down their money to watch him. It is not altogether fair to say of the modern boxer, be he out of the ordinary, that he should fight for a fixed sum. Being human, and if he is shrewd and knows that the best of his kind cannot live in the game for very long, he has his price. If a promoter comes along and is willing to pay, that is his concern. He takes a chance, as does any other business man. If much money rolls his way, he has done a good deal; if it doesn't, he burns his fingers, and nobody is going to sympathize with him.

BOXING IN THE WAR

Whether the purse given is a large or a little one, the principle is the same. There is no more morality in a small purse than there is in a fat one. If a man fights for a few pounds, he sacrifices his amateur status; in other words, he is in the game to make a livelihood. And if he gets a lot of money, good luck to him. Now, about the objection to contests on a grand scale, that is, contests to which everybody may go providing he pays. It is as clear as daylight that, in order to have a championship, someone has got to find bags of money, and if a fair return for the expenditure of that money is to be got, it is equally clear that the fight must be a public affair. The public must be free to go to it.

This the National Sporting Club has come to recognize. Obviously, they could not stage a championship that had to do with the world in Covent Garden without losing several thousands of pounds and shutting out the world from it. It would be a semi-private affair, when it should be everybody's concern. We shall all follow the National Sporting Club's venture with interest and sympathy.

And now I would tell you, among other features of boxing during the war, first about Tancy Lee, who against Danny Morgan of South Wales—one of many boys of the Principality introduced to the public by a silvery-haired gentleman named Ted Lewis, who looks after the affairs of Jimmy Wilde—made the feather-weight belt his own property. It was this Lee, it will be remembered, who as a fly-weight once beat Wilde. But on that occasion the great Jimmy was very ill, and was ill-advised to take the ring.

There was a return match, and then Wilde won in a most decisive fashion. Lee is a Scot, and because he looks so old-fashioned you would perhaps be inclined to describe him as "the old man of the woods." Quite an extraordinary little fellow is he. A year or so short of forty, he took to boxing quite late in life, but he has proved that he is the best and gamest little boxer yet reared by Scotland. He is no stylist, but he can fight, and when he was declared to have won against Morgan he received a great ovation. It was only by a very few points that he got home; all the time it was a neck-and-neck race.

The victory of Lee, which ensured the Lonsdale Belt having a permanent home in Scotland, will do incalculable good; for, the spirit of emulation being common to all boys, you may depend upon it that the Scottish lads will be after becoming another Tancy Lee.

Dick Smith took the cruiser-weight belt, and the genial Pat O'Keeffe that put up for the middles, while Tommy Noble won the trophy offered to fly-weights. O'Keeffe has retired after about as varied a career as most pugilists. I don't suppose he made a fortune out of the Ring, but, my word, he has seen things! He has boxed in different parts of the world, and was in Tommy Burns's corner when he lost to Jack Johnson (now somewhere in Spain as a sort of boxer, toreador, and wrestler) at Rushcutter's Bay.

BOXING IN THE WAR

Dick Smith, having annexed the cruiser belt, ventured against Frank Goddard, giving heaps of weight and height away. The contest took place at the Ring, Blackfriars, where Goddard, by the way, made short work of Sergeant Harold Rolph, a replica of poor Bob Fitzsimmons, and who, together with Corporal Joe Attwood and Jimmy Clarke, proved to be the best of the Canadian soldier-boxers who came over to this country.

Smith against Goddard put up what I thought to be the fight of his life. His boxing was unusually good, very different from that of Goddard, who is no boxer at all, and doesn't mind admitting it. But the boxer, as personified by Smith, was beaten by the fighter, Goddard.

I saw Goddard's fight with Joe Beckett at the National Sporting Club. Down he was sent very early in the contest by a blow that would have caused most men to quit, but he merely shook himself as would some Newfoundland puppy, and finished by compelling Beckett to retire.

Because of this I said at the time that Goddard, were he taught how to stand, how to box, how to protect himself by a carefully arranged defence, would beat everybody. But this he seemed to think unnecessary, and after he had beaten Jack Curphey at the N.S.C. he was knocked out in the third round by Beckett, at Olympia, who thus qualified to meet Carpentier.

After Beckett had disposed of Wells, I talked with

the Frenchman. Said he : " Your Joe Beckett is a hard and dangerous fighter, but if it has to be that I will be called upon to fight him at Olympia, what matters ? If when I take the ring I am as good as I was against Gunboat Smith, then I do not expect much trouble. For, Mr Corri, you will agree that Beckett had not much to beat in Wells, for Billie came into the ring as a man without legs, like a soldier who had lost them in the war. Billie did much to beat himself. He forgot how to box ; he did not know how to fight ; and so I go back to Paris certain that Beckett did not accomplish a very great deal. And about Goddard ? Oh, yes, he is a mighty fellow, but didn't you once say, Mr Corri, that the bigger the man is, the more there is to hit. So there ! "

When Carpentier reappears in the ring I am certain that it will have to be recorded that the boom of 1914 was nothing by comparison with what will happen then. I left Carpentier preparing to leave for the military school at Joinville le Pont, where he became instructor after some eighteen months' flying over the German lines and winning, as I have already said, splendid distinction.

" I shall not be long in the army," he declared, as I bade him farewell ; " and then I go into training for my first fight, which will be against your Dick Smith at Strasburg. Afterwards I expect I shall have a contest in Paris, and then in the autumn I will appear at your Olympia. If I come through, perhaps next year I will go to America and seek a fight for the world's championship. It is not likely that I shall remain in the fighting game for more than two or three years. In that time I hope to have made a second fortune. If I do, I shall settle in the country as a farmer."

Meantime not only Goddard and Beckett, but Eddie McGoorty, professed to be starving for a fight with the French champion, who, I would remark, looks none the worse for his war experiences—a little older, but still very young-looking, and a trifle taller and heavier. About matches to come—there will be no end of them. Johnny Basham, our welter-weight, is being much sought after. He is fighting almost as well as ever he did, and there can be no question that he is as near a world-beater as makes no matter.

With the eclipse of Wells—will it be a temporary eclipse ?—the most popular of all Britisher boxers is unquestionably Wilde.

Some little time ago, when it was given out that Ledoux—very much alive, though his death in action has been many times recorded—was about to be demobilized, negotiations were set on foot to match him against Wilde; but I have an idea that Jimmy will not concede so much weight to the French lad, who, if he is anything like the fighter he was against Joe Bowker and Digger Stanley, is the most ferocious little chap I know, and one that even Wilde might be excused from tackling.

I have always held that in the matter of humanity

boxing took a front place in all our sports. Of all the impelling things during the War, what we called " the American nights " at the National Sporting Club once a week appealed to me most.

Let me tell you what happened when American troops began to pour into London. James White, who was responsible for the introduction of Georges Carpentier to this country, held that the most natural thing to do was to provide them with a playground. And being a keen and deep student of human nature, he knew that the American soldier, being like our soldiers, had an inborn love for boxing. So he caused the National Sporting Club to be presented to them, lock, stock, and barrel, every Wednesday night for some eighteen weeks, and, in that thorough way typical of the real Lancastrian, set out to organize competitions for them.

Admiral Sims and General Biddell encouraged the idea for all it was worth, and there came about a once-a-week boxing carnival the like of which had never been seen before. The Club was packed from floor to ceiling every Wednesday, and very quickly we had real international bouts. Men of the Services of the world fought with gusto, and when these nights came to an end we all said that a great work had been done.

James White was presented with a mountain of a loving-cup on behalf of the men of the American navy and army, and it was no exaggeration to say —as was said—that by means of this boxing a

BOXING IN THE WAR

great and lasting brotherhood had been established. Through no other agency could a better understanding between American and British boys have been created, and perhaps without even suspecting it Mr White, helped as he was by the National Sporting Club, did the greatest possible service to boxing; for, done as he caused it to be done, the outside public saw and admitted the true meaning of the sport, the discipline it exacted and the good-fellowship it set up.

Yes, we have entered upon a new and a better boxing era. It is almost certain that it will be made a compulsory part of the training in the Services; all the public schools are bound to take it up, and surely in the very near future a full blue will be given for boxing at the universities.

We have cried and are crying for an A1 nation. The surest means to beget one is by encouragement of all sports that make for character. And boxing, from my point of view, and as the result of a long life in the game, must be practised everywhere and by everybody. Give to boxing a properly organized government, and we shall have a race of fighters, clean and chivalrous. We shall have a race of men who will be *men*.

During the War many famous and history-making pugilists passed away. John L. Sullivan, whom I knew so well, and who thought he must have made the better part of a million out of the Ring, died in comparative poverty, but well and sympathetically cared for by his friends. And Bob Fitzsimmons and

Charlie Mitchell are no more. Australia has lost probably one of its greatest of many great fighters—Les Darcy, the young blacksmith who had never known defeat. He slipped away from his home to America instead of going to war. He was not allowed to fight in the States, and he fretted so that when but a few years more than twenty he died of a broken heart.

But there are many great men to carry on. We shall not breed men like Sullivan, Fitzsimmons, Mitchell, and Darcy for some generations, may be; but as the outcome of the War, and with the wholehearted support and sympathy which is being given to boxing, we shall build up a standard of skill that will be splendidly high.

The future of boxing is assured.

AMUSEMENT FOR THE HOME.

IN STIFF PICTORIAL WRAPPERS. **Price 1/6 Net each.**

The Game of Billiards
And How to Play It.
BY JOHN ROBERTS.

With Numerous Diagrams.

CONTENTS.—The Table and Accessories—The Care of Tables and Cues—Easy Losing Hazards—Mode of Using the Rest—Strength—Kiss Cannons—Losing Hazards with Side—Some Cushion Cannons—Cannons by first striking a Cushion—Some Cushion Winning Hazards—Some Cushion Losing Hazards—Close Cannons—Six Typical Close Cushion Positions—Some Following Cannons—Some often Occurring Winning Hazards—Some Gathering Strokes—Some Useful Baulks—Some Run Through Losers—Importance of Position.

After-Dinner Sleights and Pocket Tricks.
BY C. LANG NEIL.

With upwards of 100 Illustrations.

A Collection of Amusing Tricks requiring very little skill, and no, or very simple, apparatus. These Tricks are, as the title suggests, especially suitable for a few minutes' amusement after dinner, or to fill up what might become an awkward pause, as the time occupied in the presentation of each is very short.

That's a Good Story
A Collection of 400 of the Best Anecdotes.

Selected and Edited by A. M. LEIGH.

Cloth Bound, with Picture Jacket by JOHN HASSALL.

Pearson's Humorous Reciter and Reader

Contains choice selections from the Writings of J. K. JEROME, J. M. BARRIE, F. ANSTEY, F. C. BURNAND, W. W. JACOBS, ROBERT BARR, and all the best humorous writers.

Card Tricks
Without Sleight of Hand or Apparatus.
BY L. WIDDOP.

A volume which will give the Amateur or Semi-Professional, who does not wish to spend a great deal of time in practice, material for entertaining performances. Card Tricks presented in new forms and with up-to-date patter.

Modern Card Manipulation
BY C. LANG NEILL.

With upwards of 100 Illustrations.

Contains Explanations of all the best Card Tricks of the leading Conjurors. The tricks are illustrated with actual Photographs taken at the various stages of performance, and thus the amateur is enabled to follow the methods employed with the greatest ease.

Simple Conjuring Tricks
That Anybody can Perform.
BY WILL GOLDSTON.
Second Edition.

A Splendid Collection of Tricks, with and without Apparatus, within the scope of the beginner who wishes to amuse his friends at evening parties, etc.

Conjuring with Coins
Including Tricks by NELSON DOWNS
And other well-known Conjurers.

Edited by NATHAN DEAN.

A splendid collection of Simple Tricks.

Hand Shadows
The Complete Art of Shadowgraphy.
BY LOUIS NIKOLA.

In Stiff Pictorial Wrapper, with numerous illustrations showing how the shadows are produced.

These Handbooks may be obtained through your Bookseller, or will be forwarded post free on receipt of 1s. 9d., from

C. ARTHUR PEARSON, Ltd., 17 Henrietta St., LONDON, W.C. 2.

USEFUL HANDBOOKS ON ATHLETIC SPORTS.

In Cloth Boards. Price 1s. 6d. net each; postage 3d. extra.

Association Football

By J. L. JONES,
Welsh International Twenty Times, and Captain Tottenham Hotspurs, 1901-4.

A Complete Handbook to all Departments of the Game, with Rules and Explanation of the Offside Rule.

Rugby Football

By JEROME J. RAHILLY
(*London Irish Rugby Football Club*)

A Practical Handbook of the Game and How to Play It, together with Rules, etc.

Boxing

With a Selection on Singlestick.

BY
A. J. NEWTON,
Lightweight Amateur Champion 1888 and 1890.

With 20 Illustrations.

Walking

A Practical Guide to Pedestrianism.

By C. LANG NEILL.

With Contributions by
W. J. STURGESS and W. GRIFFIN.

With Illustrations.

CONTENTS.—The Science of Walking—Walking of a Natural Kind — Athletic Walking — Walking with Bent Legs — Exertion in Walking—Training—Exercise in Training—Ages for Training—Massage, etc. — Care of the Feet — An Athlete's Clothing and Embrocation—Walking Tours—Mountaineering—Walking Records, etc., etc.

Cricket

EDITED BY
GILBERT L. JESSOP.

The Contents include Contributions by
K. S. RANJITSINHJI, C. B. FRY, G. L. JESSOP, C. L. TOWNSEND, AND GEO. BRANN.

Rowing and Sculling

By W. G. EAST,
Ex-Champion Sculler of the Thames, and Bargemaster to H.M. King Edward VII.

A thoroughly practical handbook by an expert, with 20 illustrations showing correct and incorrect positions.

Camping Out

For Boy Scouts and Others.

By VICTOR BRIDGES.

With Prefatory Note by
LT.-GEN. SIR R. BADEN-POWELL, K.C.B.

Limp Cloth.

The above volumes may be had of all Booksellers, or post free from the Publishers,
C. Arthur Pearson, Ltd., 17-18 Henrietta Street, London, W.C. 2

Printed in the United Kingdom
by Lightning Source UK Ltd.
130581UK00001B/162/A